MGA CARS

13-ISBN 978-1-84155-055-8

CONTENTS

The M.G. A Twin Cam Two-seater

A Roadworthy Sports Car of Very High Performance

ONE hundred and eight net horsepower from an unsupercharged engine of 1.6 litres swept volume is a figure which only a very short time ago would have inspired a picture of a noisy, intractable and probably temperamental racing machine. As the power (together with the disc brakes) is the feature of paramount importance in the latest M.G., one may as well sum up the car to begin with by stating that it is relatively noisy, entirely tractable, quite untemperamental and will probably appeal in the main to owners who wish to win races.

Apart from minor details of trim, these two mechanical features are the only departures made by the "Twin Cam" M.G. A from its less expensive and very well known counterpart. It seems justifiable to leave for a moment a recapitulation of familiar virtues and vices, and concentrate for once upon a straight comparison figures between the old and the new.

In respect of maximum speed a comparison with the last M.G. A tested by The Motor cannot be exact, owing to the slightly greater drag effect of a fabric hood and sidescreens. An increase in net power output of exactly 50% has however raised the mean speed by 12% and the best one-way run to a creditable 115 m.p.h., the latter figure corresponding precisely to the peak engine speed of 6,700 r.p.m. This is by no means all. It might be supposed that the main advantage of a twin overhead camshaft design would be to increase performance at the upper end of the speed range, without comparable gains at lower revolutions. The only extent to which this is true is that, with the new car running on German pump fuel of approximately 97 Octane instead of its preferred 100 Octane, the rather academic acceleration test for 10 to 30 m.p.h. in top gear had to be omitted. Thenceforward the improvement in acceleration times is so marked as to warrant a table of direct comparisons between the standing-start figures for two cars.

Rest to:			Twin Cam	Normal
30 m.p.h.	...	...	2.6 sec.	5.0 sec.
40 m.p.h.	...	...	4.4 sec.	7.2 sec.
50 m.p.h.	...	...	7.3 sec.	10.8 sec.
60 m.p.h.	...	...	9.1 sec.	15.6 sec.
70 m.p.h.	...	...	12.3 sec.	21.4 sec.
80 m.p.h.	...	...	16.2 sec.	32.1 sec.

Perhaps the most revealing way to sum up this performance is to say that of all the cars so far tested by The Motor only machines built specifically for sports-car racing would keep pace with this 1,600 c.c. touring two-seater in a standing start

match to speeds of 60, 70 or 80 m.p.h.

Observant readers will have noticed that although racing cars are excluded from this comparison the "Twin-Cam" has already been referred to as a potential winner of competitions. To what extent has racing performance been bought at the cost of inconvenience? There is, to begin with, a considerable increase in noise, both mechanically from the engine and from the tailpipe when the throttle is opened at all wide. Neither is particularly objectionable at the speeds of normal traffic, but both can become tiring with the prolonged cruising at 90 m.p.h. or so which is a very practicable possibility with this type of car.

So long as 100 Octane fuel can be obtained the engine is extremely docile at low revolutions and extremely smooth at high ones. On slightly lower grades it pinks only when pulling hard at low speeds, but has a very definite tendency to run-on after the ignition has been switched off. A fairly rich mixture setting of the twin S.U. carburetters was indicated by the fact that after a mild night under cover there was no need of the "choke" for starting, although steady speed fuel consumption tests bear out the reasonable economy achieved in fast Autobahn cruising. Under typical English conditions, indirect gears and high engine speeds are used as a matter of course to hustle the M.G. from point to point, and treatment of this sort has to be paid for. A check over 170 miles, using a good deal of full-throttle acceleration with a rev. limit of between 5,500 r.p.m. and 6,000 r.p.m., showed a fraction under 20 m.p.g., which

In Brief

Price (including oil cooler, as tested) £854 10s. plus purchase tax £428 12s. equals £1,283 2s.

Capacity	...	...	1,588 c.c.
Unladen kerb weight	...		19½ cwt.

Acceleration:
20-40 m.p.h. in top gear ... 10.7 sec.
0-50 m.p.h. through gears 7.3 sec.

Maximum direct top gear gradient ... ... 1 in 9.3
Maximum speed ... ...113.0 m.p.h.
"Maximile" speed ... ...101.3 m.p.h.
Touring fuel consumption ... 27.6 m.p.g.
Gearing: 17.2 m.p.h. in top gear at 1,000 r.p.m.; 19.4 m.p.h. at 1,000 ft./min. piston speed.

Accessibility is not the strongest point of the new and appreciably more bulky engine. The distributor cannot be reached without removing the heater air duct, just visible to the right of the top radiator hose. The camshaft covers are chrome-plated.

Cockpit layout is unchanged from the normal M.G. A., but the seats are more heavily padded and better shaped, while the instrument panel is covered in leather.

The M.G. A Twin Cam Two-Seater

puts a sharp restriction on the range of a 10-gallon fuel tank. Different styles of driving, on the other hand, do not appear to affect an oil consumption in the region of one pint for every 120 miles. The test car was fitted with the external oil cooler which is an optional extra, and which lies between the radiator and grille.

To continue the review of new features, the highest praise can be given to the Dunlop disc brakes, which are fitted in conjunction with centre-lock, perforated steel disc wheels. Really high average speeds, whether on busy motor roads or ordinary fast highways, make demands upon a braking system quite different from those of day-to-day driving. Consistent performance from disc brakes is by no means universal, yet the Dunlops combine smooth and progressive action right down to zero speed with a reassuring ability to slow the M.G. quite abruptly from 100 m.p.h. as often as small saloons hold their course in the fast lane of an Autobahn—which can be very frequently. They appear, moreover, to be unaffected by rain as well as heat.

Having dealt with those components by which, in return for some £180 of basic price, the owner of the "Twin Cam" M.G. obtains a considerable edge over his fellows, it would not be quite accurate to say that the car as supplied for test was in other respects just like its predecessor. The M.G. A has built up an enviable reputation for roadholding and sensitive handling, largely because it

is, so to speak, stronger than it is fast. It must be recorded that the faster model, after 500 miles in England and 1,000 on the Continent, was virtually without front shock absorbers and suffering accordingly. In particular quite severe scuttle shake and reaction through the steering wheel would build up at speeds between about 70 m.p.h. and 85 m.p.h.

Whilst the shock absorbers are operative—and presumably after a more robust pattern has been adopted—the handling of the car is in the excellent M.G. A tradition. The steering is neither especially light nor especially heavy, but absolutely positive and responsible in a manner which is rare. Just sufficient understeer is present to make the car straight running and insensitive to cross-winds, without requiring efforts of skill or strength on a winding road. The cornering power of the new Dunlop Road Speed RS4 tyres is exceptional on a dry surface, provided that higher pressures are adopted than the 18 lb. front and 20 lb. rear recommended

Space in the boot is limited by the necessity to fit in a spare wheel, but a couple of soft grips can be carried without much difficulty. On top of the wheel is a full set of tools.

for "normal" driving—at least 24 lb. and 26 lb. seems to be desirable. In the wet these tyres favour enterprising use of the accelerator if corners are to be taken fast, when the rear wheels break away very easily, but at the same time very controllably. The embarrassing and much more dangerous phenomenon of a front-wheel slide is happily unknown to the M.G. driver.

Stated thus baldly, the plain facts of roadholding behaviour may not convey to a reader unfamiliar as yet with the M.G. A its most endearing characteristic: that of being fun to drive. This quality as a whole is hard to pin down, yet instantly recognizable by anyone coming fresh to the car, and is probably owed to the obvious but not universal circumstance of a set of controls which all work perfectly. The steering and brakes have been remarked upon. An essential of any sports car is a really good gearbox and that of the M.G. is first class, with a light and completely positive movement of the short lever but no obstruction to snatched changes from the synchromesh. The only objections are a reverse position located

5

The hood, although rather cumbersome to erect, is extremely efficient in keeping out rain and draughts. Centre-lock pressed steel wheels are standard equipment.

next to second and therefore provided with rather too strong a guard spring for convenience, and a biggish gap between the second and third ratios which allow speeds of approximately 81 and 50 m.p.h. respectively at 6,500 r.p.m. The clutch is completely without slip, and befits a car which will readily spin its wheels during getaway on a dry road. The accelerator, in spite of a flexible cable connection, works well and is placed so that it is easy to blip the throttle with the side of the foot to synchronize engine and transmission speeds while braking.

In a car with slower steering, requiring more arm work, the bucket seats might be uncomfortably close up to the steering wheel even for the long-legged. As it is, shorter drivers move in a rather restricted space, but the seats themselves are comfortable, well padded, more upright than most and excellent in holding the driver in place. At medium tyre pressures—high enough to ensure good roadholding, but below the 30-32 lb. requested for maximum runs—the suspension provides a much more comfortable ride than might be expected of so solid-feeling a car, possibly on account of softer sidewalls in the new tyres. Even over really bad pave, jarring through the steering wheel was the only unpleasant sensation.

The seats are fairly low slung between the chassis side-rails, with the advantage of greater protection against the elements from high doors and the corresponding disadvantage of slightly reduced visibility. Nevertheless, any driver tall enough to see over the scuttle has a clear view of both front wings, while transparent panels now sewn into the hood fabric allow almost 350-degree vision even when it is raised. The latter operation is one requiring a good deal of perseverance for one man to complete it in less than four or five minutes, although the hood offers the compensation of being one of the most weatherproof of its kind when erect. No drop of water entered in quite heavy rain, and the windscreen is kept well clear outside by electric wipers and inside by a powerful fresh-air heater and demister. Plated studs on the scuttle, for attaching the tonneau cover, produce rather trying reflections in the windscreen.

Stowage of the hood, complete with its folding frame, behind the seats, considerably reduces the limited space available for luggage, the greater part of the boot (whose lid is released by a concealed toggle inside the car) being occupied by the spare wheel and tools. A couple of soft grips, together with small articles which can be wedged into odd spaces or the door pockets, just about complete the possible payload when two people are carried. It would appear that an enterprising accessory manufacturer might produce a lockable glove box to make use of the part of the facia panel now occupied alternatively by a decorative emblem or the optional car radio controls.

Quarts into pint pots frequently take up a lot of the available space. The extra width of a twin o.h.c. cylinder head has filled the bonnet to very near its capacity, and the engine is by no means as accessible as formerly. The dipstick, requiring as it does frequent attention, is almost completely hidden from view; a fault which could be most easily cured by fitting a long tube rising to the top of the engine. Similarly the distributor cannot be reached at all without first uncoupling the air duct to the interior heater.

The "Twin Cam" M.G. A is not intended for very large scale production, and such details as these may well be unimportant to the comparatively few people who, by their choice of the more costly model, indicate that performance is their first consideration. When one or two matters have been attended to there is little doubt that numerous competition successes will come the way of the M.G., the more so because of its favourable situation in the 1,600 c.c. category.

Specification

Engine

Cylinders	4
Bore	75.4 mm.
Stroke	89.0 mm.
Cubic capacity	1,588 c.c.
Piston area	27.7 sq. in.
Valves	Overhead (twin o.h.c.)
Compression ratio	9.9/1
Carburetters	Two S.U. H6
Fuel pump	S.U. electric
Ignition timing control	Centrifugal and vacuum
Oil filter	Tecalemit full flow
Max. power (net)	108 b.h.p.
at	6,700 r.p.m.
Piston speed at max. b.h.p.	3,910 ft./min.

Transmission

Clutch	Borg and Beck 8 in. s.d.p.
Top gear (s/m)	4.3
3rd gear (s/m)	5.908
2nd gear (s/m)	9.520
1st gear	15.652
Reverse	20.468
Propeller shaft	Hardy Spicer open
Final drive	Hypoid
Top gear m.p.h. at 1,000 r.p.m.	17.2
Top gear m.p.h. at 1,000 ft./min. piston speed	19.4

Chassis

Brakes	Dunlop disc
Friction lining area	32 sq. in.
Suspension:	
Front	Coil springs and wishbones
Rear	Semi-elliptic
Shock absorbers:	
Front and rear	Armstrong lever
Steering gear	Cam Gears rack and pinion
Tyres	Dunlop Road Speed 5.90-15 tubed

Coachwork and Equipment

Starting handle	Yes
Battery mounting	One each side behind seats
Jack	Screw
Jacking points	No fixed points
Standard tool kit:	3 double-ended spanners, 4 box spanners, tommy bar, feeler gauge, grease gun, adjustable spanner, pliers, Phillips screwdriver, tool roll, wheel nut hammer, screwdriver, tyre pump.
Exterior lights:	2 head, 2 side/indicator, 2 stop/tail/indicator, rear number plate.
Number of electrical fuses	2
Direction indicators	Flashing, self-cancelling
Windscreen wipers	Lucas electric
Windscreen washers	Optional, Tudor
Sun vizors	None
Instruments:	Speedometer with decimal trip distance recorder, rev. counter, oil pressure gauge, fuel gauge, water thermometer.
Warning lights:	Indicators, dynamo charge, headlamp main beam.

Locks:		
With ignition key		Ignition only
With other keys		None
Glove lockers		None
Map pockets		Two in doors
Parcel shelves		One behind seats (with hood up)
Ashtrays		Optional
Cigar lighters		Optional
Interior lights		Optional
Interior heater	Optional, Smiths 3½kw. fresh air type	
Car radio	Optional, Radiomobile	
Extras available:	Heater and demister, cold air ventilation, cigar lighter, adjustable steering column, luggage grid, wing mirror, tonneau cover, radiator blind, horn, foglamp, radio, competition windscreen, ashtray, windscreen washer, hardtop, sliding sidescreens, badge bar, sun vizor, seats, oilcooler, tonneau cover.	
Upholstery material	Leather and leathercloth	
Floor covering		Carpet
Exterior colours standardized		Five
Alternative body styles		Coupe

Maintenance

Sump	12 pints, S.A.E. 30 (below 32° F. S.A.E. 20)	
Gearbox	4 pints, S.A.E. 30	
Rear axle	2¼ pints, S.A.E. 90 (extreme cold, S.A.E. 80)	
Steering gear lubricant	S.A.E. 90 oil (extreme cold, S.A.E. 80)	
Cooling system capacity	13¾ pints (1 drain tap)	
Chassis lubrication	By grease gun every 1,000 miles to 9 points	
Ignition timing	t.d.c.	
Contact-breaker gap	0.015 in.	
Sparking plug type	Champion No. 3	
Sparking plug gap	0.024-0.026 in.	
Valve timing: Inlet opens 20° b.t.d.c., closes 50° a.b.d.c.; exhaust opens, 50° b.b.d.c., closes 20° a.t.d.c.		

Tappet clearances (hot)		
Inlet		0.018 in.
Exhaust		0.018 in.
Front wheel toe-in		Nil
Camber angle		1°
Castor angle		4°
Steering swivel pin inclination		9°
Tyre pressures:		
Normal, Front		18 lb.
Rear	20 lb. (see text)	
Fast, Front		22 lb.
Rear		24 lb.
Competition, Front		24 lb.
Rear		26 lb.
Brake fluid		Lockheed No. 103
Battery type and capacity	Lucas SG9E 12v., 51 amp./hr.	

The **Motor** Road Test No. 22/58 (Continental)

Make: M.G.   **Type:** M.G. A Twin Cam Two-seater
Makers: M.G. Car Co., Ltd., Abingdon-on-Thames, Berkshire.

Test Data

World copyright reserved; no unauthorized reproduction in whole or in part.

CONDITIONS: Weather: Warm and dry, light wind. (Temperature 52°-61° F., Barometer 30.0-30.1 in. Hg.) Surface: Dry concrete Autobahn (acceleration and maximum speed tests). Dry concrete banked track for fuel consumption tests.
Fuel: German pump fuel, approx. 97 Research Method Octane Number (acceleration and maximum speed tests), 100 R.M.O.N. elsewhere.

INSTRUMENTS
Speedometer at 30 m.p.h.	2% fast
Speedometer at 60 m.p.h.	6% slow
Speedometer at 90 m.p.h.	4% slow
Distance recorder	3% slow

WEIGHT
Kerb weight (unladen, but with oil, coolant and fuel for approx. 50 miles)... ... $19\frac{1}{2}$ cwt.
Front/rear distribution of kerb weight $53\frac{1}{2}/46\frac{1}{2}$
Weight laden as tested ... ... 23 cwt.

MAXIMUM SPEEDS
Flying Quarter Mile
Mean of four opposite runs ... ...113.0 m.p.h.
Best one-way time equals ... ...115.0 m.p.h.

"Maximile" Speed. (Timed quarter mile after one mile accelerating from rest.)
Mean of four opposite runs ... ...101.3 m.p.h.
Best one-way time equals ... ...104.2 m.p.h.

Speed in Gears. (at 6,500 r.p.m. recommended limit).
Max. speed in 3rd gear ... ... 81 m.p.h.
Max. speed in 2nd gear ... ... 50 m.p.h.
Max. speed in 1st gear ... ... 31 m.p.h.

FUEL CONSUMPTION
Top gear
37 m.p.g. at constant 30 m.p.h. on level.
$36\frac{1}{2}$ m.p.g. at constant 40 m.p.h. on level.
$33\frac{1}{2}$ m.p.g. at constant 50 m.p.h. on level.
$32\frac{1}{2}$ m.p.g. at constant 60 m.p.h. on level.
$29\frac{1}{2}$ m.p.g. at constant 70 m.p.h. on level.
$26\frac{1}{2}$ m.p.g. at constant 80 m.p.h. on level.
22 m.p.g. at constant 90 m.p.h. on level.
$17\frac{1}{2}$ m.p.g. at constant 100 m.p.h. on level.

Overall Fuel Consumption for 1,593 miles, 71.7 gallons, equals 22.2 m.p.g. (12.7 litres/100 km.).

Touring Fuel Consumption (m.p.g. at steady speed midway between 30 m.p.h. and maximum, less 5% allowance for acceleration) 27.6.
Fuel tank capacity (maker's figure) 10 gallons.

STEERING
Turning circle between kerbs:
Left ... ... 31 feet
Right ... ... 30 feet
Turns of steering wheel from lock to lock $2\frac{3}{4}$

BRAKES from 30 m.p.h.
0.90g retardation (equivalent to $33\frac{1}{2}$ ft. stopping distance) with 100 lb. pedal pressure.
0.80g retardation (equivalent to $37\frac{1}{2}$ ft. stopping distance) with 80 lb. pedal pressure.
0.51g retardation (equivalent to 59 ft. stopping distance) with 50 lb. pedal pressure.
0.32g retardation (equivalent to 94 ft. stopping distance) with 25 lb. pedal pressure.

TRACK FRONT 3'-11½" REAR 4'-0½"   OVERALL WIDTH 4'-10"
20"   10"   SCALE 1:50   GROUND CLEARANCE 6"   7'-10"   13'-0"   4'-2"   20½"   10½"   M.G.A TWIN-CAM

SCREEN FRAME TO FLOOR 35½"   SEAT TO HOOD 38"
11¼"   41½"   26¼"   11½"   32½"   15"   23   10½"   18½"   47   8½"   21   18½"
28" DOOR WIDTH
NOT TO SCALE   STEERING WHEEL ADJUSTABLE 3¼"

ACCELERATION TIMES from standstill
0-30 m.p.h.	...	...	...	2.6 sec.
0-40 m.p.h.	...	...	...	4.4 sec.
0-50 m.p.h.	...	...	...	7.3 sec.
0-60 m.p.h.	...	...	...	9.1 sec.
0-70 m.p.h.	...	...	...	12.3 sec.
0-80 m.p.h.	...	...	...	16.2 sec.
0-90 m.p.h.	...	...	...	24.6 sec.
0-100 m.p.h.	...	...	...	40.3 sec.
Standing quarter mile	...	...		18.1 sec.

ACCELERATION TIMES on upper ratios
			Top gear	3rd gear
10-30 m.p.h.			—	8.3 sec.
20-40 m.p.h. ...	...	...	10.7 sec.	6.5 sec.
30-50 m.p.h. ...	...	...	9.7 sec.	6.5 sec.
40-60 m.p.h. ...	...	...	8.8 sec.	5.5 sec.
50-70 m.p.h. ...	...	...	9.4 sec.	5.5 sec.
60-80 m.p.h. ...	...	...	13.9 sec.	8.3 sec.
70-90 m.p.h. ...	...	...	15.2 sec.	—
80-100 m.p.h....	...	...	23.1 sec.	—
90-110 m.p.h....	...	...	—	—

HILL CLIMBING at sustained steady speeds
Max. gradient on top gear   1 in 9.3 (Tapley 240 lb./ton)
Max. gradient on 3rd gear   1 in 6.6 (Tapley 335 lb./ton)
Max. gradient on 2nd gear   1 in 4.0 (Tapley 545 lb./ton)

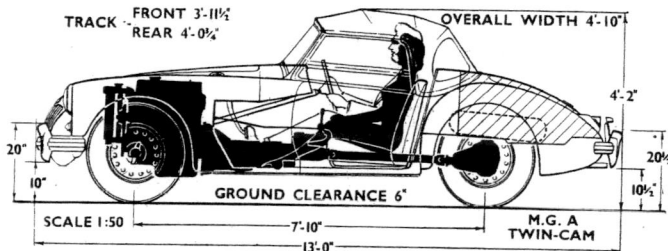

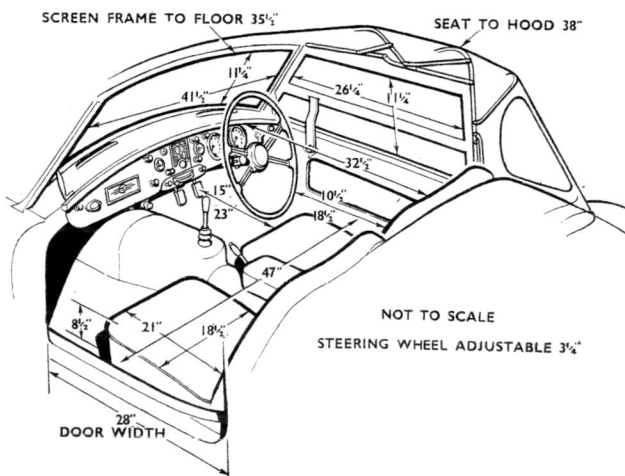

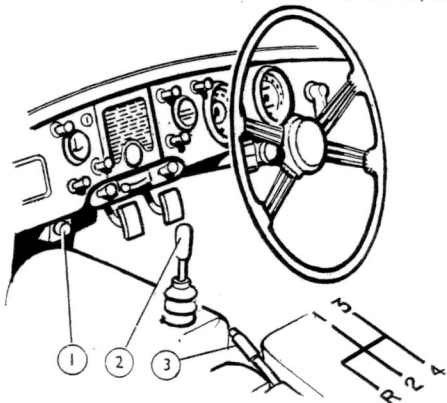

1, Headlamp dip switch. 2, Gear lever. 3, Handbrake. 4, Bonnet catch release. 5, Fuel contents gauge. 6, Windscreen washer button. 7, Choke control. 8, Ventilator control. 9, Heater control and fan switch. 10, Horn button. 11, Demister control. 12, Starter switch. 13, Water thermometer. 14, Dynamo charge warning light. 15, Trip resetting knob. 16, Headlamp main beam indicator. 17, Map reading light switch. 18, Map reading light. 19, Windscreen wipers switch. 20, Ignition switch. 21, Oil pressure gauge. 22, Lights switch. 23, Foglamp switch. 24, Rev. counter. 25, Panel light switch. 26, Speedometer and distance recorder. 27, Direction indicator switch. 28, Direction indicator warning light.

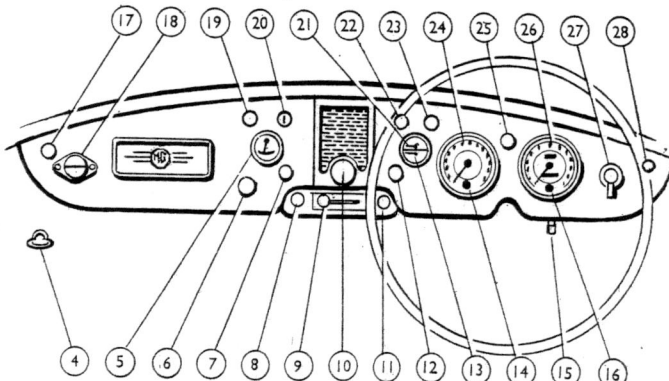

The M.G. A 1600 Two-Seater

Extra Acceleration and Retardation for a Popular Sporting Car

FAMILIAR since the autumn ot 1955 as a sporting two-seater of notable strength and roadworthiness, the M.G. A has now been endowed with extra acceleration by an increase in cylinder bore, and with improved retardation by disc-pattern Lockheed front brakes. Involving no price increase whatever, and accompanied by other minor refinements, these two important changes increase the attractiveness of what is already a very popular model.

Enlargement of the engine by 6½% without any alteration in the 4.3/1 axle ratio has produced a welcome improvement in the acceleration of the M.G. A which extends throughout its speed range. From 30 m.p.h. to 50 m.p.h. in top gear, the latest car took 10.6 sec., whereas the original M.G. A of September 1955 took 11.4 sec., and the M.G. A Coupé which we tested in August 1957 took 13.8 sec.; from 50 to 70 m.p.h. the latest car takes 13.3 sec. as against 14.9 sec. for the 2-seater in 1955 and 13.7 sec. for the hardtop in 1955. Acceleration from a standstill through the gears benefits very markedly from the extra engine torque, rest to 50 m.p.h. and 70 m.p.h. times of 9.1 sec. and 17.7 sec. comparing with 10.8 sec. and 21.9 sec. for the earlier 2-seater, 10.8 sec. and 21.4 sec. for the former coupé.

It may at first glance seem surprising that the engine changes which have resulted in such markedly improved acceleration through the gears have not raised the top speed of the car. With full silencing as installed in the car, however, the new engine develops peak power at 5,300 r.p.m. corresponding to approximately 89-90 m.p.h. in top gear, the timed mean speed of just over 96 m.p.h. being well within the 6,000 r.p.m. limit suggested by a red sector on the tachometer dial but 7% beyond the peak of the power curve. Raised tyre pressures, and/or the use of Road Speed tyres which are an optional extra, in place of the tubeless touring-quality tyres fitted to our test model, would no doubt have reduced drag and lifted the top speed—so, judging by our experience of other M.G. cars, would some additional running-in of an engine which was quiet mechanically and used very little oil indeed. What matters about the M.G. A 1600 is not, however, its ultimate speed, but the ease and rapidity with which 80 m.p.h. can be reached and exceeded whenever there is a slight break in the traffic on ordinary main roads.

Complete docility characterizes the enlarged engine, as witness our recording of top gear acceleration times from a mere 10 m.p.h., and it runs happily on ordinary Premium grades of petrol without demanding 100-octane, but it does not feel to pull its full weight below 2,500 r.p.m. In the warm summer weather which prevailed during our test, the choke was never needed for starting from cold, even after the car had stood in the open throughout rainy nights. The engine can seem rather harsh when accelerated hard in the gears, an effect which is difficult to define exactly as neither exhaust nor mechanical noise levels are high for a sports car. Fuel economy proved rather inferior to smaller-engined preceding models, our checks showing between 23½ m.p.g. and 25½ m.p.g. in varied (but always fast) road driving.

In Brief

Price £663 plus purchase tax £277 7s. 6d., equals £940 7s. 6d.

Capacity		1,588 c.c.
Unladen kerb weight ...		18¼ cwt.
Acceleration:		
20-40 m.p.h. in top gear ...		11.0 sec.
0-50 m.p.h. through gears		9.1 sec.
Maximum top gear		
gradient		1 in 10.9
Maximum speed ...		96.1 m.p.h.
"Maximile" speed ...		94.1 m.p.h.
Touring fuel consumption ...		29.7 m.p.g.

Gearing: 17.0 m.p.h. in top gear at 1,000 r.p.m.; 29.1 m.p.h. at 1,000 ft./min. piston speed.

COMFORT and convenience have been well studied in the layout and equipment of the cockpit; the two bucket seats have a central armrest between them on the propeller-shaft tunnel, just to the rear of the short gear lever. Rev. counter and speedometer are two large circular dials immediately in front of the driver, with smaller dials for fuel gauge, oil pressure and water thermometer on the left.

The Motor Road Test No. 21/59

Make: M.G. **Type: M.G. A 1600**

Makers: M.G. Car Co., Ltd., Abingdon-on-Thames, Berkshire.

Test Data

World copyright reserved; no unauthorized reproduction in whole or in part.

CONDITIONS: *Weather: Warm and dry, gusty 10 m.p.h. cross wind. (Temperature 59°-63° F., Barometer 29.6-29.7 in. Hg.) Surface: Dry tar macadam and concrete. Fuel: Premium grade pump petrol (approx. 96 Research Method Octane rating).*

INSTRUMENTS
Speedometer at 30 m.p.h.	accurate
Speedometer at 60 m.p.h.	3% fast
Speedometer at 90 m.p.h.	4% fast
Distance recorder	accurate

WEIGHT
Kerb weight (unladen, but with oil, coolant and fuel for approx. 50 miles) .. 18¼ cwt.
Front/rear distribution of kerb weight 53/47
Weight laden as tested .. .. 22 cwt.

MAXIMUM SPEEDS
Flying Lap of Banked Circuit .. .. 96.1 m.p.h.
Best one-way ¼-mile on straight .. 100 m.p.h.

"Maximile" Speed (Timed quarter mile after one mile accelerating from rest).
Mean of four opposite runs .. .. 94.1 m.p.h.
Best ¼ mile time equals .. .. 96.3 m.p.h.

Speed in Gears (at 6,000 r.p.m. recommended limit).
Max. speed in 3rd gear .. .. 74 m.p.h.
Max. speed in 2nd gear .. .. 46 m.p.h.
Max. speed in 1st gear .. .. 28 m.p.h.

FUEL CONSUMPTION
39½ m.p.g. at constant 30 m.p.h. on level
37 m.p.g. at constant 40 m.p.h. on level
34½ m.p.g. at constant 50 m.p.h. on level
32 m.p.g. at constant 60 m.p.h. on level
29¼ m.p.g. at constant 70 m.p.h. on level
27 m.p.g. at constant 80 m.p.h. on level
23 m.p.g. at constant 90 m.p.h. on level

Overall Fuel Consumption for 1,028 miles, 42.2 gallons equals 24.4 m.p.g. (11.6 litres/100 km.).

Touring Fuel Consumption (m.p.g. at steady speed midway between 30 m.p.h. and maximum, less 5% allowance for acceleration) 29.7 m.p.g.
Fuel tank capacity (maker's figure) 10 gallons.

STEERING
Turning circle between kerbs:
Left .. .. 29½ ft.
Right .. .. 28¼ ft.
Turns of steering wheel from lock to lock 2¾

BRAKES from 30 m.p.h.
1.00 g retardation (equivalent to 30 ft. stopping distance) with 100 lb. pedal pressure.
0.82 g retardation (equivalent to 36¾ ft. stopping distance) with 75 lb. pedal pressure.
0.53 g retardation (equivalent to 56¾ ft. stopping distance) with 50 lb. pedal pressure.
0.29 g retardation (equivalent to 104 ft. stopping distance) with 25 lb. pedal pressure.

TRACK: FRONT 3'-11½" / REAR 4'-0½"
OVERALL WIDTH 4'-10"
4'-2"
20° / 10° / 20½" / 10½"
GROUND CLEARANCE 6"
SCALE 1:50 — 7'-10" — 13'-0"
M.G. A 1600

SCREEN FRAME TO FLOOR 35½" SEAT TO HOOD 38"
NOT TO SCALE
STEERING WHEEL ADJUSTABLE 3½"
DOOR WIDTH 28"

ACCELERATION TIMES from standstill
0-30 m.p.h.	4.3 sec.
0-40 m.p.h.	6.4 sec.
0-50 m.p.h.	9.1 sec.
0-60 m.p.h.	13.3 sec.
0-70 m.p.h.	17.7 sec.
0-80 m.p.h.	25.1 sec.
Standing quarter mile	19.8 sec.

ACCELERATION TIMES on Upper Ratios
	Top gear	3rd gear
10-30 m.p.h.	12.1 sec.	8.0 sec.
20-40 m.p.h.	11.0 sec.	6.9 sec.
30-50 m.p.h.	10.6 sec.	6.8 sec.
40-60 m.p.h.	11.2 sec.	7.4 sec.
50-70 m.p.h.	13.3 sec.	9.0 sec.
60-80 m.p.h.	15.0 sec.	—

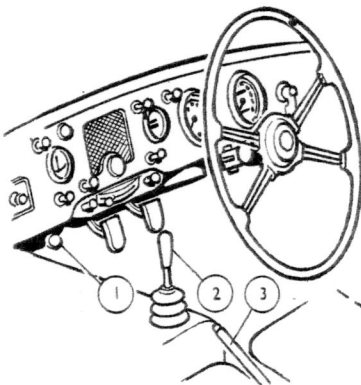

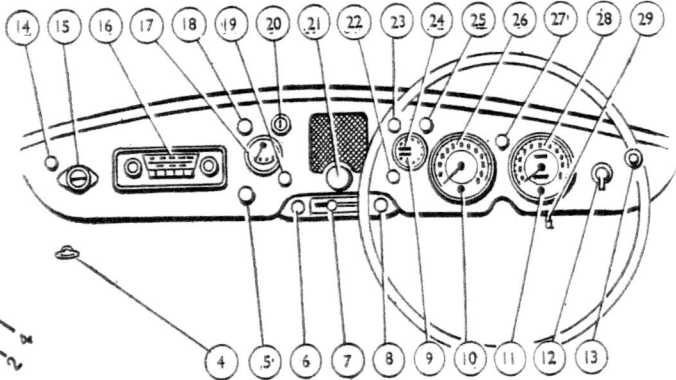

HILL CLIMBING at sustained steady speeds
Max. gradient on top gear	1 in 10.9 (Tapley 205 lb./ton)
Max. gradient on 3rd gear	1 in 7.3 (Tapley 305 lb./ton)
Max. gradient on 2nd gear	1 in 4.5 (Tapley 485 lb./ton)

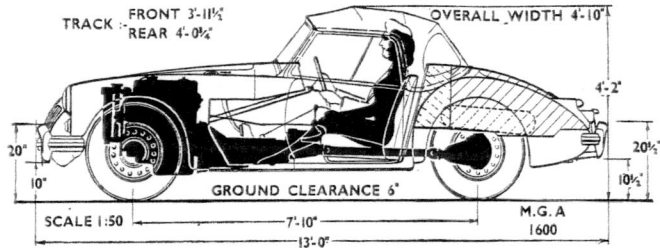

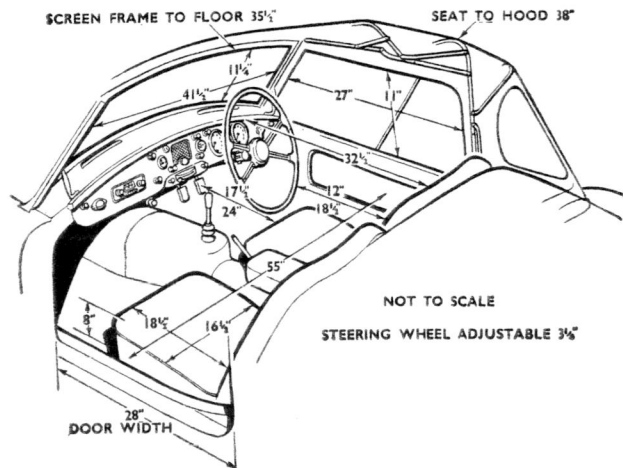

1, Headlamp dipswitch. 2, Gear lever. 3, Handbrake. 4, Bonnet catch release. 5, Windscreen washer button. 6, Heater air-intake control. 7, Heater temperature control. 8, Demister control. 9, Water thermometer. 10, Dynamo charge warning light. 11, Headlamp main beam indicator lamp. 12, Direction indicator switch. 13, Direction indicator warning light. 14, Map-reading light switch. 15, Map-reading light. 16, Radio controls. 17, Fuel contents gauge. 18, Windscreen wipers switch. 19, Choke control. 20, Ignition switch. 21, Horn button. 22, Starter button. 23, Lights switch. 24, Oil pressure gauge. 25, Switch for optional fog-lamp. 26, Tachometer. 27, Panel light rheostat. 28, Speedometer and distance recorder. 29, Trip adjuster.

Provision of Lockheed 11-inch disc brakes behind the bolt-on front wheels has given this car an immense reserve of stopping power. There is outstandingly good balance between front and rear brakes, so that the car can be checked from 95 m.p.h. down to a standstill at virtually the limit of tyre adhesion without any fuss or excitement whatever. An extended series of stops from 60 m.p.h., at the closest intervals permitted by very good acceleration, produced no perceptible fade but merely a slight and entirely temporary loss of the usual perfect balance between the four brakes. As we have noted on some other disc-braked cars, a form of brake squeal could be induced by extremely gentle brake application at town speeds, a trivial price to pay for smoothly progressive stopping power which inspired utter confidence at all times. The fly-off hand-brake works very effectively upon the rear drums, location of the pull-up lever on the right of the transmission tunnel being reasonably convenient for tall drivers but awkward when the driving seat was adjusted further forwards.

Apart from the new braking system, no chassis changes in this model have been announced, nor was there any reason to expect them. Exceptional strength characterizes a box-section frame of which the scuttle structure is an integral part, and although 18¼ cwt. is thought rather heavy for a 1.6-litre sports 2-seater, stamina is known to go with the appreciable weight, and if the gearbox is used properly, acceleration can be very brisk indeed. Factory recommendations on the subject of tyre

ALTHOUGH the smooth bonnet falls away to a very low front, the engine compartment is not cramped and access for routine maintenance is good.

pressures cover rather a wide range, but we found the highest recommended pressures to be best suited to everyday use of this sporting car, which otherwise took town corners to an accompaniment of loud tyre squeal.

Even with quite high tyre pressures, the coil-spring I.F.S. and semi-elliptic rear springs are very far from harsh, and in fact a certain amount of body roll is evident during fast cornering, despite the low build of the M.G. A. Around town, there is not quite the same cushioned ride as

HOLDING the spare wheel, the boot has room only for soft luggage; those contemplating serious touring can obtain a grid to fit the boot lid.

many present-day touring cars provide, but the suspension is extremely well suited to comfortably "flat" riding at the brisk pace which is natural to this car on country roads of all kinds. There is certainly no cause to be shy of taking the M.G. A onto really rough surfaces.

Like other M.G. two-seaters for a considerable number of years past, this model has a rack-and-pinion steering gear which is extremely positive in action, without any of the backlash or flexibility which spoil the precision of all too many steering installations based upon worm or screw gearing. In conjunction with a chassis which seems never to "put a foot wrong," steering gear precision makes this a very brisk car from point to point, especially on the secondary roads which in Britain often serve as traffic avoiders.

At the extremes of the speed range, it must be noted that the fully reversible rack-and-pinion steering, slightly damped by a friction device which makes it self-adjusting for wear, does reveal shortcomings. Below 25 m.p.h. the friction is evident enough to cause a slight amount of "wander," and above 60 m.p.h. road reac-

tion begins to reach the driver's hands, of small amplitude but persistent enough to leave his fingers tingling after a fast non-stop hundred miles. Whilst it has strong self-centering action, the steering never becomes very heavy, and a turning circle of below 30 feet diameter is extremely convenient on many occasions.

Set just about as conveniently close to the steering wheel rim as it could possibly be without getting in the way is the knob of a central remote-control gear lever, controlling an excellent four-speed gearbox. Faults can be found with the transmission, some people finding the small across-the-gate movement needed for a 3rd-to-2nd change awkward at first, and others tending to make audible changes into top gear when in a hurry, due to not depressing the clutch pedal through the whole of its travel. With familiarity these points cease

o- Seater

DISTINGUISHED from earlier models by rigid sliding side-screens and deeper plinths to accommodate flasher units separate from the rear lamps, the M.G. A 1600 retains such useful features as a large rear window and quarter lights in the hood, stout bumpers and smooth, easy-to-clean bodywork.

to obtrude, but a rather wide gap between 3rd and 2nd gears (which, at the 6,000 r.p.m. where a red sector of the tacho-meter begins, respectively, give speeds of about 74 m.p.h. and 45 m.p.h.) remains evident, the designers presumably not wishing changes down into an unsynch-ronized 1st gear to be needed very often. But, regardless of these imperfections, the smoothly firm clutch and quiet, easy-to-use gearbox are thoroughly appropriate to the car.

Purely and simply a two-seater, the sleek body of this car is no more difficult to enter than most comparable low-built models. The floor is flat and the doors open down to floor level, but the sturdy structure of the car does not let the doors extend far enough forward for utmost ease of entry. Once entered, this car offers an exceptionally high standard of comfort and convenience, the individual seats with their "wrap around" backrests having an adjustment range which even the very tall find satisfactory. Between the seats, a cushioned armrest covers the propeller shaft tunnel, and hollowed-out doors provide quite generous elbow width in the cockpit as well as two very capacious pockets. The facia is a metal panel onto which instruments and controls have been crowded with little pretence at "styling" but with a great deal of practical common sense—the speedometer and matching tachometer face the driver directly, a combined oil pressure gauge and coolant thermometer is close beside them and the fuel gauge

not far away. Unusual but convenient once a driver is accustomed to them, are facia-panel locations of the horn button (on the driver's left) and turn-indicator time switch (on the driver's right), the horn button being touch-sensitive so that either a gentle cautionary note or a strident warning can be given at will. Rheostat-controlled lighting is provided for the instruments, a map reading light is in front of the passenger, and a spare switch is provided for a foglamp if this extra is specified.

All-weather equipment takes the form of two sidescreens and a hood, all of which can in fine weather be stowed safely and invisibly behind the seats. These removable items really do keep out wet weather, and stay firmly in place at the car's maximum speed—the curved-glass windscreen has bracing struts which serve also as grab handles, the hood fastens to the windscreen at three points, and when the doors are closed, rubber-cushioned fittings on the sidescreens hold them in rattle-free contact with the windscreen. Each sidescreen has a sliding half panel to provide ventila-

tion, and in striking contrast with the one-time austerity of sporting cars is the inclusion of a fresh air cockpit heater and windscreen de-mister in this competitively-priced model's extensive range of optional built-in extras.

The two criticisms which must be made of the hood are, that the car becomes very much noisier to drive when it is in use owing to wind-induced flutter of the roof fabric, and that the multiple joints which let a really rigid hood frame fold away so neatly make reasonably rapid erection or folding of the hood a skilled task. By some people's standards of judgement, the luggage locker also is criticized as being of rather modest size.

With its share of the imperfections from which no car ever altogether escapes, this remains a very attractive and versatile sporting two-seater. Sturdy, well furnished and probably built with more thorough care than most of its contemporaries, it travels fast and is enjoyable to drive or ride in, yet can also serve as a reliable and weatherproof form of everyday transportation.

Specification

Engine

Cylinders	...	4
Bore	...	75.39 mm.
Stroke	...	88.9 mm.
Cubic capacity	...	1,588 c.c.
Piston area	...	27.68 sq. in.
Valves	...	Push-rod o.h.v.
Compression ratio	...	8.3/1
Carburetters	...	Twin S.U. type H4
Fuel pump	...	S.U. electrical
Ignition timing control	...	Vacuum and centrifugal
Oil filter	Full flow Tecalemit or Purolator	
Max. power (net)	...	75.5 b.h.p.
at	...	5,300 r.p.m.
Piston speed at max. b.h.p.	3,090 ft./min.	

Transmission

Clutch	...	Borg and Beck 8 in. s.d.p.
Top gear (s/m)	...	4.3
3rd gear (s/m)	...	5.908
2nd gear (s/m)	...	9.520
1st gear	...	15.652
Reverse	...	20.468
Propeller shaft	...	Hardy Spicer, open
Final drive	...	Hypoid bevel
Top gear m.p.h. at 1,000 r.p.m.	...	17.0
Top gear m.p.h. at 1,000 ft./min. piston speed	...	29.1

Chassis

Brakes	...	Lockheed hydraulic—disc front, drum rear
Brake diameter	...	Disc 11 in., drum 10 in.
Friction lining area	...	87 sq. in.
Suspension:		
Front	...	Independent coil springs and wishbones
Rear	...	Rigid axle with half-elliptic leaf springs
Shock absorbers	...	Armstrong, hydraulic lever arm
Steering gear	...	Rack and pinion
Tyres	...	Dunlop 5.60—15 tubeless

Coachwork and Equipment

Starting handle	Yes
Battery mounting	One each side behind seats
Jack	Screw-type
Jacking points	Front wishbones and rear springs

Standard tool kit: Jack, wheelbrace and hub cap lever (combined), starting handle, 1 box and 3 open-ended or box spanners, sparking plug spanner, tommy bar, cylinder head spanner, ring-type tappet spanner, adjustable spanner, tappet feeler gauge, screwdriver grease gun, tyre pump, No. 2 screwdriver, pliers, brake bleeder tube, distributor screw-driver and gauge, tyre lever, tyre valve spanner, rear axle drain plug key, tool roll.

Exterior lights	2 head, 2 side, 2 stop and tail
Number of electrical fuses	2
Direction indicators	Flashing type, self-cancelling
Windscreen wipers	Electrical two-blade, self-parking
Windscreen washers	Optional
Sun vizors	None
Instruments:	Speedometer with decimal trip recorder, tachometer, oil pressure gauge, water temperature gauge, fuel gauge.
Warning lights	Dynamo charge, turn indicators, headlamp main beam

Locks:		
With ignition key	...	Ignition switch
With other keys	...	None
Glove lockers	...	None
Map pockets	...	In each door
Parcel shelves	...	None
Ashtrays	...	None
Cigar lighters	...	None
Interior lights	...	Instrument panel

Interior heater: Optional extra: Smith's 3½ kW. fresh-air-type with de-misters.

Car radio	...	Optional, H.M.V.

Extras available: Heater, radio, wire wheels, whitewall tyres, 5.90—15 Road Speed tyres, alternative 4.55:1 axle ratio, adjustable steering column, tonneau cover, radiator blind, twin horns, anti-roll bar, fog lamp battery cover, badge bar, screen washers, detachable hardtop, competition windscreen, luggage carrier, wing mirror, cold air ventilation, ashtray, competition de luxe seats.

Upholstery material: Leather on wearing parts, leathercloth borders.

Floor covering	...	Carpet
Exterior colours standardized	...	6
Alternative body styles:	Fixed-head coupe or detachable hardtop	

Maintenance

Sump	8 pints, S.A.E. 30 (winter 20W)
Gearbox	4½ pints, S.A.E. 30
Rear axle	2 pints, S.A.E. 90 Hypoid
Steering gear lubricant	90 Hypoid
Cooling system capacity	10 pints (2 drain taps)
Chassis lubrication	By grease gun every 1,000 miles to 10 points
Ignition timing	6° b.t.d.c.
Contact-breaker gap	0.015 in.
Sparking plug type	Champion N5
Sparking plug gap	0.025 in.

Valve timing: Inlet opens 16° b.t.d.c. and closes 56° a.b.d.c.; exhaust opens 51° b.b.d.c. and closes 21° a.t.d.c.

Tappet clearances (hot)	Inlet and exhaust 0.015 in.
Front wheel toe-in	Parallel
Camber angle	¼°-1°
Castor angle	4°
Steering swivel pin inclination	9°-10½°
Tyre pressures:	
Front	17-23 lb.
Rear	20-26 lb. (according to speed)

Brake fluid Lockheed grade 103 (S.A.E. 70-R-1)
Battery type and capacity: Two 6-volt Lucas SG9E, 51 amp. hr.

The M.G. Series-M.G.A. Two-seater

An Uncommonly

Roadworthy

1½-litre Sports

Car of High

Performance

Individual modern styling marks the new M.G.—and more than that. At 60 m.p.h. the M.G.A. requires 27% less power to maintain its speed than the TF Midget. Hood and sidescreens continue the smooth shape as far as is possible.

CARS, like people, are in their varying degrees martyrs to fashion, and whether the current dictates of fashion are a good or a bad thing sometimes makes little difference. Some are brought up to date almost year by year to embody the very latest in everything, others hold out until the very last before falling into line with the majority, and a few, after a period of resistance, change their fashion only for a new one entirely their own.

It is to the last group, oddly enough, that the M.G. "A" two-seater (described in *The Motor*, September 28, 1955) belongs. The new car has, to be sure, a smooth and good-looking body whose lines follow contemporary style, and a performance which

puts it at least on a competitive footing with the smaller fast sports cars to which we have become accustomed. There, however, the resemblance virtually ends, for alongside the small machines with moderately stressed engines of 2 or more litres there is now a car of comparable size with an engine capacity of 1,489 c.c. The fact is, of course, of primary importance to the competitions driver as putting the car in the 1½-litre class; aside from competition, there are virtues in a small (and therefore light), engine which will be mentioned again later.

In its essence the M.G.A although not in title a "Midget," is still small; it is compact, manoeuvrable and lively, regards the carriage of luggage as secondary to the sport of motoring, and responds to its driver's wishes in a way the larger car can seldom hope to do except at much greater expense.

However good its intangible qualities, it is by performance that a sports car will inevitably be judged in the first instance, and the figures recorded on the opposite page, which were established as usual on the Belgian motor road, provide all the assurance that may be needed that the car can hold its own in good company. On the noisy side mechanically in com-

parison with present-day touring designs, the M.G. engine was prone to run-on if switched off quickly after a fast drive, but was otherwise tolerant of all premium-grade fuels. The exhaust note will obviously please many buyers, its loudness increasing progressively with engine speed and throttle opening.

The special significance of a return to 1½ litres for a sports car lies in re-teaching an old lesson that the smaller the proportion of weight, and within limits the less the actual weight on the front wheels of a car, the more responsive will be its "handling"—a comprehensive term which needs no elucidation to the enthusiast. It will be seen that the M.G., without driver but ready for the road and with a small quantity of fuel in the tank, has some 53% of its weight carried by the front wheels, or only a few pounds more on the front than the back, while the position of seats and fuel tank ensures that the greater part of any additional load will bear on the back wheels. The total weight of the pre-production model supplied for test, which in contrast to subsequent production models had aluminium panelled doors and bonnet and boot lids, may raise a few eyebrows in a theoretical appraisal of power-weight ratios, but the majority verdict amongst

In Brief

Price: £595 plus purchase tax £249 0s. 10d. equals £844 0s. 10d.

Capacity	...	...	1,489 c.c.
Unladen kerb weight	...		18¼ cwt.
Fuel consumption	...	...	26.7 m.p.g.
Maximum speed	...	...	97.8 m.p.h.

Maximum speed on 1 in 20
gradient ... ... 80 m.p.h.

Maximum top gear gradient 1 in 13.7

Acceleration:
10-30 m.p.h. in top ... 11.0 sec.
0-50 m.p.h. through gears 10.8 sec.

Gearing: 17.0 m.p.h. in top at 1,000 r.p.m.; 72.8 m.p.h. at 2,500 ft. per min. piston speed.

The M.G. Series - M.G.A. - Contd.

High-sided, the cockpit is unusually draught-free even in its most open condition. Instruments are where they should be, and the horn button on the facia M.G.-fashion. Forethought is shown by windscreen struts which do double-duty as grab handles.

pedal with too long a travel for heel-and-toe downward gear changes to be made.

There are, on the other hand, no half measures about the brakes. Ten-inch drums with a friction lining area of 134 sq. in. not only show excellent results on a Tapley meter with moderate pressure, but were almost unaffected by a series of deliberate hard applications in the rapid descent of a long French main road hill. If under extreme conditions further brake cooling were ever necessary, it should be provided by the wire wheels which are

the several members of our staff who drove the car was that the extra pounds put into a superlatively strong and rigid chassis were weight well spent.

To drive the M.G.A. on a winding open road is sheer enthusiast's delight. Rack and pinion steering and small cars have always gone well together, and the lightness of the steering with a small, four-spoked wheel is matched by a quickness and precision which might not be expected from the lock-to-lock figure (for a very compact lock) of 2¾ turns. In this case the secret lies in an admirable example of useful and controllable oversteer. In point of fact an improvement in the handling was found possible by inflating the tyres from the recommended fast-driving pressures of 18 lb. front and 23 lb. for the rear wheels to approximately 26 lb. on all four. The effect of the oversteer then was merely that the driver, rather like a pilot in some types of aircraft, steered into a turn and then virtually centralized the wheel to keep the car on its course. It was notable that to some tastes at least the extra sponginess of the tyres at lower pressures did not make

for a more comfortable ride, and had the further disadvantage of causing tyre squeal on corners, otherwise entirely absent.

Quite apart from steering characteristics, the cornering power of the car is extremely good, holding it down in a manner to give the driver complete confidence, and seeming almost indifferent to the type of road surface. As is often the case a wet road gives an earlier indication of the car's behaviour when pressed to the limit on a corner, sliding of the rear wheels beginning quite gradually and being easily transformed into a controlled drift. Wheelspin is very quickly provoked in starting from rest in the wet, due possibly to the combination of a small, high-revving engine and a throttle control which on the left-hand drive model under test was awkward in the extreme. It is an unfortunate thing that a sports car should have its throttle opened by an enclosed cable (which is the same on left- or right-hand drive models), and a small source of joy to the sporting driver is denied him by an accelerator

optional equipment for the M.G. An effective fly-off handbrake lever is placed horizontally on the right-hand side of the transmission tunnel, convenient with right-hand drive but on a left-hand drive car close to the passenger's legs.

Like the brakes, the clutch is hydraulically operated by a hanging pedal, and most surprisingly is smooth even to the point of slipping under really brutal treatment. It may be observed that the latter was very much a feature of our acceleration tests, since the gearbox synchromesh was good enough to allow full-throttle "snatch" changes upwards through all the gears. The M.G. Company have always had a good name for the handiness of their remote-control gear levers, and this model is no exception, although an almost universal complaint amongst drivers, admittedly unused to changing gear with their right hands, was a difficulty in moving quickly from third to second gear. If the choice of ratios can be criticized it is in a second gear equivalent to only 42 m.p.h. at the maxi-

Power beneath a low bonnet has been obtained with practically no sacrifice of accessibility, excepting only the batteries which are carried behind the seats. The distributor is just out of sight below the sparking plugs.

Shallow and very much occupied by spare wheel and tools, the boot can carry a couple of soft grips if need be. A grid for more awkward luggage is an available accessory.

Less noise but still quite good weather protection is obtained with hood up and side-screens stowed away. Visibility to the rear is reasonable through a wide plastics window.

mum recommended engine speed of 5,500 r.p.m., but the willingness of the engine to rev freely up to and even occasionally beyond this limit largely makes up for the restriction. In the light of modern practice it is often a surprise to cruise in top-gear comfort and then discover that the engine is turning over at 4,500 r.p.m., and some form of higher gear is a tantalizing consideration for the long distance motorist.

Driving Position

Although the ride itself is remarkably comfortable, low slung seats result in a driving position needing a straight and unbraced left leg and a right knee (this again in the left-hand drive car), which, owing to proximity of the steering wheel rim, would have been happier with a universal joint, while all the assorted shapes of The Motor staff found a lack of support for the small of the back. The seats nevertheless are well sprung and well covered in leather, and excellently shaped to prevent passengers being flung about in fast cornering. The central bulge over the transmission is covered with padded leather. The low build ensures that tall drivers do not find themselves in the slipstream above the curved windscreen, which throws the airstream well to the side of the cockpit, and sidescreens with spring-hinged lower sections can help to make the car yet more snug even when open. Some advantage is indeed to be gained by driving in this trim in anything less than rain or snow, particularly if the very powerful heater is fitted, as the level of noise in the cockpit rises a great deal with the hood in place.

Mundane matters of convenience must weigh to some extent with the most sporting of car owners, and the virtues which largely give the M.G. its personality have been bought to some extent at the expense of creature comfort. To raise or even to lower the hood single-handed is an exercise in skill and patience, so that the full-length tonneau cover proved a most valuable "extra" on the test car. The space left free behind the seats when the hood is erect will,

however, take a fair number of parcels, which might otherwise have to be left at home. The sidescreens are normally carried in separate compartments of a bag in this space, and the spare wheel on the floor of the luggage locker. Tools in a large roll are strapped on top of the spare wheel, leaving enough luggage room for two canvas grips and smaller objects, but scarcely for hard suitcases. The list of extra items available for the car includes an external luggage carrier for the boot lid, one of which was fitted to the test car and proved rather frail. Maps, torches and the rest of the small oddments which go with travelling find a home in open door pockets.

Circular instrument dials, with markings which have suffered a little at the stylist's hands, are grouped where they may be easily seen by the driver; speedometer, rev counter, water thermometer and oil pressure and fuel gauges are included, but no ammeter. The distinctive M.G. feature of a convenient horn button on the centre of the facia is preserved. Lights, starter, choke, windscreen wipers and a map-reading light for the passenger are controlled by pull-out switches, and a manual windscreen washer is part of the optional equipment. The accessibility of the engine and chassis for maintenance or servicing, often a question of personal interest to the driver of this type of car, is uniformly good with the sole and outstanding exception of the batteries; placed on either side of the car behind the seats, they can only be inspected on removal of a plate which is itself obstructed until the spare wheel is unclamped from the boot.

Lest there be any risk, however, of a number of small notes of criticism leaving a false impression, the newest M.G. must be summed up as enthusiastically as it was everywhere received. That the modern styling is generally approved there can be no doubt, but far more important is the introduction of a small car with a degree of roadworthiness high by any standards. The famous slogan of the factory has indeed never been better applied.

Mechanical Specification

Engine

Cylinders	4
Bore	73.025 mm.
Stroke	89 mm.
Cubic capacity	1,489 c.c.
Piston area	25.97 sq.in.
Valves	Pushrod o.h.v.
Compression ratio	8.3/1
Max. power	68 b.h.p.
at	5,500 r.p.m.
Piston speed at max. b.h.p.	3,210 ft. per min.
Carburetters ...	2 inclined S.U. 1½-in.
Ignition	12-volt coil
Sparking plugs ...	14 mm. Champion NA8
Fuel pump ...	S.U. electrical, rear-mounted
Oil filter	...Full-flow Tecalemit

Transmission

Clutch	Single dry plate
Top gear (s/m)	4.3
3rd gear (s/m)	5.908
2nd gear (s/m)	9.52
1st gear	15.652
Propeller shaft	Open
Final drive	Hypoid bevel
Top gear m.p.h. at 1,000 r.p.m.	17.0
Top gear m.p.h. at 1,000 ft./min. piston speed	29.1

Chassis

Brakes	Lockheed hydraulic (2 l.s. front)
Brake drum diameter	10 in.
Friction lining area ...	134.4 sq. in.
Suspension:	
Front ...	Coil and wishbone, i.f.s.
Rear	Semi-elliptic
Shock absorbers:	
Front ...	Armstrong incorporated in upper wishbone pivots
Rear	Armstrong hydraulic
Tyres	Dunlop 5.60—15

Steering

Steering gear	Rack and pinion
Turning circle (between kerbs):	
Left	30¾ ft.
Right	28¼ ft.
Turns of steering wheel, lock to lock	2¾

Performance factors (at laden weight as tested):

Piston area, sq. in. per ton ...	24.1
Brake lining area, sq. in. per ton	125
Specific displacement, litres per ton mile...	2,440
Fully described in The Motor. September 28, 1955	

Coachwork and Equipment

Bumper height with car unladen:	
Front (max.) 18 in., (min.) 9½ in.	
Rear (max.) 21 in., (min.) 12½ in.	
Starting handle	Yes
Battery mounting	Behind seats
Jack	Screw-type
Jacking points ...	Front wishbones and rear springs
Standard tool kit: Ring-type tappet spanner, wheelbrace (copper hammer with wire wheels), tappet gauge, sparking plug spanner, pliers, grease gun, adjustable spanner, 2 tyre levers, cylinder head nut spanner, tyre valve spanner, distributor screwdriver and gauge, tyre pump, 3 box spanners, 3 o/e spanners, screwdriver, recessed screwdriver, tommy bar, jack, brake bleeder tube, gearbox plug spanner, touch-up paint pencil, tool roll.	
Exterior lights: 2 head, 2 side-indicator, 2 rear/brake/indicator.	
Direction indicators: Flashing type, self-cancelling.	
Windscreen wipers ...	Electric, self-parking
Sun vizors	No
Instruments: Speedometer with decimal trip distance recorder, rev. counter, oil pressure gauge, water thermometer.	
Warning lights ...	Ignition, indicators, headlamp main beam
Locks:	
With ignition key	Ignition
With other keys	None
Glove lockers	None
Map pockets	2
Parcel shelves	None
Ashtrays	None
Cigar lighters	None
Interior lights ...	Instrument panel, map-reading light
Interior heater	Re-circulating or fresh-air type with de-mister
Car radio	Optional, H.M.V.
Extras available: Radio, heater, wire wheels, fog lamp, whitewall tyres, 4.55/1 axle gears, twin horns, external luggage carrier, overall tonneau cover, radiator blind, rim embellishers, telescopic steering column.	
Upholstery material Leather over foam rubber	
Floor covering	Carpet
Exterior colours standardized: Black, Orient red, Tyrolite green, Glacier blue, Old English white.	
Alternative body styles	None

The **Motor** Road Test No. 23/55 (Continental)

Make : M.G. **Type : M.G.A. Two-Seater**
Makers : M.G. Car Co., Ltd., Abingdon-on-Thames.

TRACK:— FRONT 3'—11½"
REAR 4'—0¾"
SEATS ADJUSTABLE
OVERALL WIDTH 4'—10"
4'—2"
GROUND CLEARANCE 6"
7'—10"
13'—0"
M.G. SERIES M.G.A.
SCALE 1:50

FLOOR TO HOOD 42"
SCREEN FRAME TO FLOOR 35½"
SEAT TO HOOD 37½"
11½"
41"
12"
27"
32½"
18"
23"
48"
6½"
12"
17"
17½"
19"
28"
DOOR WIDTH
NOT TO SCALE

Test Data

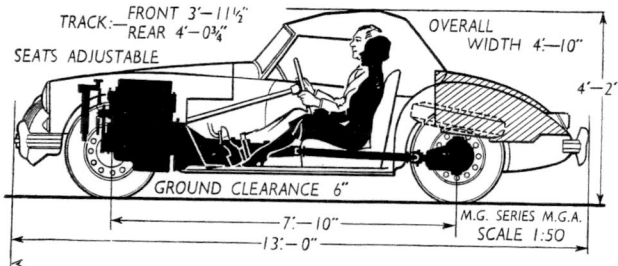

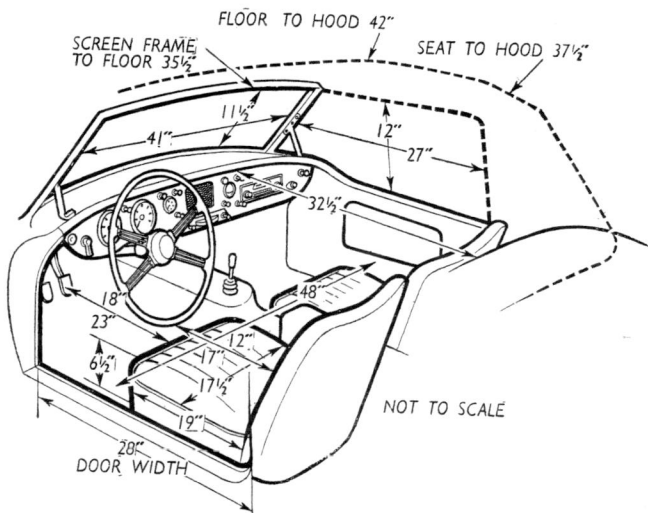

CONDITIONS. Weather . Hot with light wind (temperature 55°-75°F., barometer 29.9-30.0 in.) Surface : dry tarmac and concrete (Ostend-Ghent motor road). Fuel : British and Belgian premium petrol. Tested with hood and sidescreens erect.

INSTRUMENTS
Speedometer at 30 m.p.h	2% fast
Speedometer at 60 m.p.h.	7% fast
Speedometer at 90 m.p.h.	6% fast
Distance recorder	Accurate

MAXIMUM SPEEDS
Flying Quarter Mile
Mean of four opposite runs	97.8 m.p.h.
Best time equals	98.4 m.p.h.

Speed in gears (at recommended maximum 5,500 r.p.m).
Max. speed in 3rd gear	68 m.p.h
Max. speed in 2nd gear	42 m.p.h
Max. speed in 1st gear	26 m.p.h

FUEL CONSUMPTION
44 m.p.g. at constant 30 m.p.h.
44 m.p.g. at constant 40 m.p.h.
41 m.p.g. at constant 50 m.p.h.
38 m.p.g. at constant 60 m.p.h.
33 m.p.g. at constant 70 m.p.h.
26½ m.p.g. at constant 80 m.p.h.
21½ m.p.g. at constant 90 m.p.h.
Overall consumption for 941 miles 35.3 gallons =26.7 m.p.g. (10.6 litres/100 km.).
Fuel tank capacity 10 gallons.

ACCELERATION TIMES Through Gears
0-30 m.p.h.	4.9 sec.
0-40 m.p.h.	6.8 sec.
0-50 m.p.h.	10.8 sec.
0-60 m.p.h.	16.0 sec.
0-70 m.p.h.	21.9 sec.
0-80 m.p.h.	30.0 sec.
0-90 m.p.h.	44.6 sec.
Standing Quarter Mile	20.4 sec.

ACCELERATION TIMES on Two Upper Ratios
	Top	3rd
10-30 m.p.h.	11.0 sec.	8.6 sec.
20-40 m.p.h.	11.7 sec.	7.8 sec.
30-50 m.p.h.	11.4 sec.	7.8 sec.
40-60 m.p.h.	14.0 sec.	8.4 sec.
50-70 m.p.h.	14.9 sec.	9.6 sec.
60-80 m.p.h.	14.7 sec.	—
70-90 m.p.h.	21.4 sec.	—

WEIGHT
Unladen kerb weight	18½ cwt.
Front/rear weight distribution	53/47
Weight laden as tested	21½ cwt

SCALE B
23/55(C)
APPROX. H.P. AT DRIVING WHEELS
FUEL CONSUMPTION AT STEADY SPEED—GALLONS PER 1,000 MILES
POWER AVAILABLE
FUEL CONSUMPTION
POWER REQUIRED
M.P.H.

Drag at 10 m.p.h	33 lb.
Drag at 60 m.p.h.	100 lb.

Specific Fuel Consumption when cruising at 80% of maximum speed (i.e 78.2 m.p.h.) on level road, based on power delivered to rear wheels .. .. .. 0.74 pints/b.h.p./hr

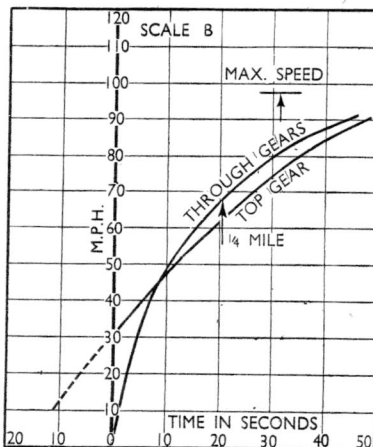

HILL CLIMBING (At steady speeds)
Max. top gear speed on 1 in 20	80 m.p.h.
Max. top gear speed on 1 in 15	67 m.p.h.
Max. gradient on top gear	1 in 11.1 (Tapley 200 lb./ton)
Max. gradient on 3rd gear	1 in 7.5 (Tapley 295 lb./ton)
Max. gradient on 2nd gear	1 in 4.8 (Tapley 465 lb./ton)

BRAKES at 30 m.p.h
0.96g retardation	(=31½ ft. stopping distance) with 95 lb. pedal pressure
0.83g retardation	(=36½ ft. stopping distance) with 75 lb. pedal pressure
0.52g retardation	(= 58 ft. stopping distance) with 50 lb. pedal pressure
0.30g retardation	(=100 ft. stopping distance) with 25 lb. pedal pressure

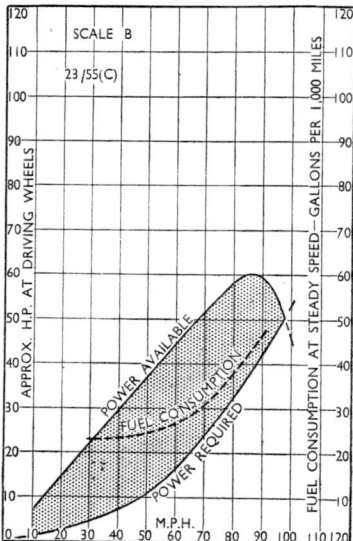

SCALE B
MAX. SPEED
THROUGH GEARS
TOP GEAR
¼ MILE
M.P.H.
TIME IN SECONDS

Maintenance

Sump : 6½ pints, S.A.E. 30. **Gearbox :** 4 pints, S.A.E. 30. **Rear axle :** 2¾ pints, Hypoid 90. **Steering gear :** Hypoid 90. **Radiator :** 10 pints (2 drain taps). **Chassis Lubrication :** By grease gun every 1,000 miles to 9 points. **Ignition timing :** 7° B.T.D.C. **Spark plug gap :** .019-.021 in. **Contact breaker gap :** .014-.016 in. **Valve timing :** I.O. 16° B.T.D.C. ; I.C. 56° A.B.D.C. ; E.O. 51° B.B.D.C. ; E.C. 21° A.T.D.C. **Tappet clearances:** (Hot) .017 in. **Front wheel toe-in :** Nil. **Camber angle :** 1°. **Castor angle :** 4°. **Tyre pressures :** Front, 17 lb., rear, 20 lb. (fast driving, 18 lb. and 23 lb.) (see text). **Brake fluid.** Lockheed. **Battery :** Lucas SG9E, 12-v. **Lamp bulbs :** Head, 42/36 w. Side/indicator. 21/6 w. rear/indicator/stop, 21/6 w.

M.G.

"M.G.A."—1956-1959

NOTE: All dimensions are in inches unless otherwise specified

TUNE UP

GENERAL.

Engine type: 4-cylinder, O.H.V. Nominal bore: 2.875. Stroke: 3.500. Cubic capacity: 90.88 cu. ins. (1,489 c.c.). Compression ratio: 8.3 to 1.

PLUGS.

Champion NA8, later N5. 14 mm. Plug gap: .024 to .026.

DISTRIBUTOR.

Lucas type DM2/P4. Service number 40488A. Contact point gap: .014 to .016. Initial timing: 7° B.T.D.C. Firing order: 1, 3, 4, 2. Minimum advance: 11° to 13° at 1,500 r.p.m. Intermediate advance: $\frac{1}{2}$° to $2\frac{1}{2}$° at 300 r.p.m. and 6° to 8° at 650 r.p.m. There is no advance under 150 r.p.m.

VALVES.

Clearance: .017 inlet and exhaust, hot.

CARBURETTER.

Twin S.U. type H4. Choke diameter: $1\frac{1}{2}$ inches. Standard needle: GS. Jet: .090. Piston spring: Red.

CAPACITIES (Imperial).

Engine, including filter: 8 pints (9.6 U.S.). Gearbox: 4 pints ($4\frac{3}{4}$ U.S.). Rear axle: $2\frac{3}{4}$ pints ($3\frac{1}{4}$ U.S.).

TYRES.

5.60-15. Standard pressures, front 17 lbs., rear 20 lbs. For faster motoring and competition work these pressures should be increased.

OIL FILTER.

Full flow type with throw-away element. When changing an element make quite sure that the seating washer for the oil filter body is in good condition.

BATTERY.

Check condition.

ELECTRICAL.

Check operation of all lamps, including stop lamps. Check windscreen wiper and other items. Check heater.

FUEL PUMP.

S.U. electric high pressure type. Delivery test 10 gallons per hour. Suction lift 33 inches. Output lift 48 inches.

TORQUE FIGURES
(IN POUNDS FEET)

Cylinder head: 50. Main bearing nuts: 70. Connecting rod setscrews: 35. Clutch assembly to flywheel: 50. (See M.G. "Magnette" for further figures.)

TOP OVERHAUL

VALVES.

Seat angle: 45°. Head diameter, inlet $1\frac{1}{2}$ inches, exhaust $1\frac{9}{32}$. Stem diameter $\frac{11}{32}$. Running clearance .0015 to .003. Valve rocker clearance for timing: .060.

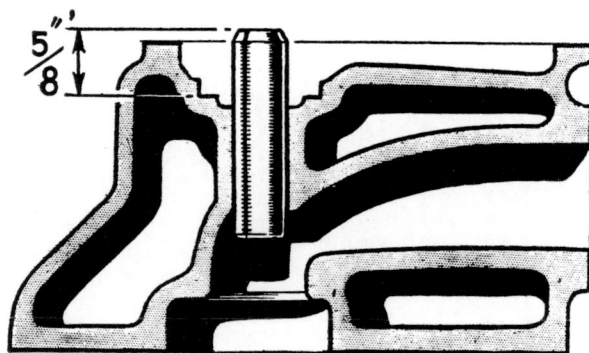

Fig. 1.—Showing the correct fitting of a valve guide.

Fig. 2.—The correct order of tightening and slackening the cylinder head retaining nuts.

The rocker gear can be removed as a complete unit but this is not a straightforward operation because the rocker retaining nuts are also the cylinder head holding down nuts. In this case the water must be drained from the cooling system, and the cylinder head nuts slackened so that the rocker gear may be removed.

Note that there is a grub screw locating the rocker shaft in the rear rocker mounting bracket. There is a plug at the forward end of the rocker shaft which may be removed for cleaning the internal oil passages.

CYLINDER HEAD.

There is no special procedure for removal except that all nuts must be slackened part of a turn at a time. Note that the cylinder head nuts also hold the brackets for the rocker gear.

Tighten nuts to 50 lbs. ft.

Note that the cylinder head gasket is marked "Front" and "Top". The copper side must always be placed upwards.

When tightening up the nuts for the cylinder head tighten the 11 nuts in the order shown in Fig. 2, and then finally tighten the remaining four rocker nuts.

When the engine has attained its normal working temperature the cylinder head nuts must be checked again.

CHECK ITEMS.

Plugs, distributor, carburetter and valves in "Tune Up".

NOTES.

Firing order 1, 3, 4, 2.

At engine number 5504 the pushrods were modified. The modification consisted of increasing the diameter of the ball end of the pushrod and also the spherical seat in the cam follower. New parts are interchangeable.

ENGINE

CYLINDER BORES AND CRANKSHAFT.

Standard cylinder bore is 2.875 with a first over-size of .010. Maximum oversize is .040.

When fitting new pistons selective assembly is necessary, and to facilitate this the pistons are stamped with identification figures on their crowns. Four grades of piston are provided for the standard bore and there is a range of four oversize pistons similarly graded.

Piston Marking					Suitable Bore Size
Standard 1	.....	......	.....		2.8745
					2.8748
2		......	.....	......	2.8749
					2.8752
3	.....			......	2.8753
					2.8756
4		......	.....	......	2.8757
					2.8760
Oversize +.010	.....	......		......	2.8845
					2.8848
+.020	.....	......			2.8945
					2.8948
+.030	.....	......		......	2.9045
					2.9048
+.040	.....	......	.....		2.9145
					2.9148

Pistons suitable for a standard bore are marked on their crowns with a grade number ranging from 1 to 4, each enclosed in a diamond, e.g., a piston stamped with a figure 2 should be fitted to a standard bore bearing a similar stamp. Oversize pistons are marked with the actual oversize dimensions enclosed in an ellipse. A piston stamped .020 is only suitable for a bore .020 larger than the standard bore; similarly, piston with other markings are only suitable for the oversize bore indicated.

The piston grading marks indicate the actual bore size to which they must be fitted, the requisite clearance being allowed for in the machining.

After reboring an engine, or whenever fitting pistons differing in size from those removed during dismantling, ensure that the grade or size of the piston fitted is stamped clearly on the top of the cylinder block alongside the appropriate cylinder bore.

Pistons are supplied in the sizes indicated in the table.

Crankshaft main journal diameter 2.000. Minimum regrind diameter 1.96. Crankpin journal diameter 1.875. Minimum regrind on crankpin 1.835. Crankshaft end thrust is taken by washers at the centre main bearing, end float being .002 to .003. Running clearance of main bearings .0005 to .002.

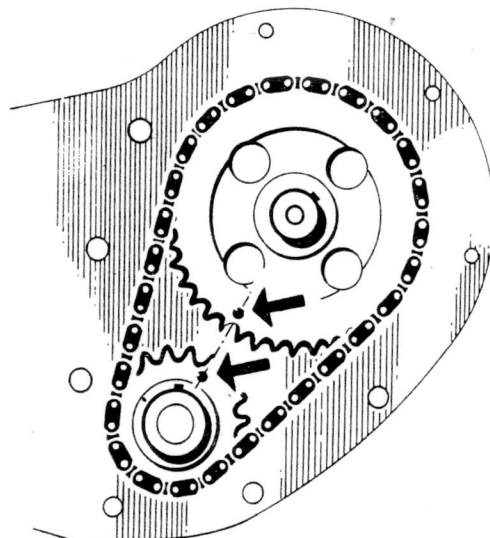

Fig. 3.—When replacing the chain wheels the timing marks indicated by the arrows must be in line to give correct valve timing.

PISTONS AND CONNECTING RODS.

For full details of piston sizes for various cylinder bores see the table in "Cylinder Bores and Crankshaft".

The big end bearings are made of steel and lead indium. Bearing side clearance .008 to .012. Bearing running clearance .0001 to .0016.

The oil control ring is the slotted type with a width of .1552 to .1562. Thickness .111 to .118. Fitted gap .008 to .013. Groove clearance .0016 to .0036.

The gudgeon pin is clamped in the little end of the connecting rod. Fit in the piston is .0001 to .00035. This is a hand push at 68°F. Diameter .6869 to .6871.

Pistons and connecting rods come up through the top of the cylinder block.

Note when re-assembling that the connecting rod big ends are offset.

VALVES, GUIDES AND SPRINGS.

Valve timing is checked and set by dimples on the timing wheels.

Inlet opens 16° B.T.D.C. Inlet closes 56° A.B.D.C. Exhaust opens 51° B.B.D.C. Exhaust closes 21° A.T.D.C. Valve guide length, inlet $1\frac{7}{8}$, exhaust $2\frac{9}{32}$. Diameter, inlet .3438 inside and .5635 outside, exhaust .3438 inside and .5635 outside. Fitted height above the cylinder head .625.

Valve spring free length, inner $1\frac{31}{32}$, outer $2\frac{3}{64}$. Fitted length, inner $1\frac{7}{16}$, outer $1\frac{9}{16}$. Pressure with the valve open, inner 50 lbs., outer 105 lbs. With the valve closed, inner 30 lbs., outer $60\frac{1}{2}$ lbs.

TAPPETS, ROCKERS AND CAMSHAFT.

Tappet type, flat base. Diameter $1\frac{3}{16}$. Diameter at the working face $\frac{9}{16}$. Length 2.293 to 2.303.

Rocker bush, outside diameter .751. Rocker arm bore .7485 to .7489. Inside diameter of rocker bush when it is reamed in position .616 to .620.

Camshaft journal diameter, front 1.78875 to 1.78925, centre 1.72875 to 1.72925, rear 1.62275 to 1.62325. End float .003 to .007. Camshaft bearing outside diameter before fitting, front 1.920, centre

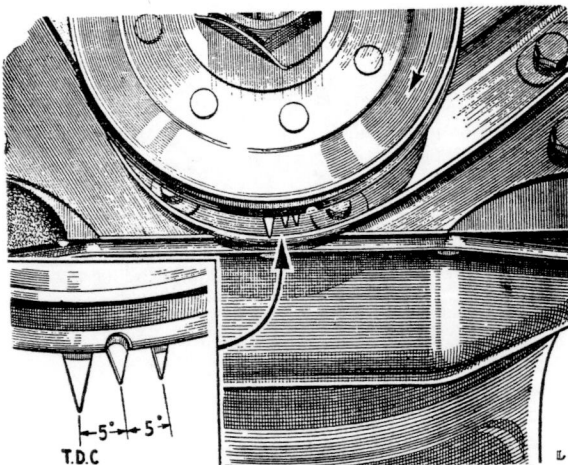

Fig. 5.—Replacing the distributor drive spindle with the aid of a tappet cover bolt. Notice the slot angle. The large offset is towards the front of the engine.

1.860, rear 1.754. Inside diameter of bush after reaming, front 1.790, centre 1.730, rear 1.624. Camshaft running clearance .001 to .002.

LUBRICATING SYSTEM.

The oil pump is the eccentric rotor type and the relief valve opens at 75 to 80 p.s.i. The relief valve spring free length is 3 inches, fitted length $2\frac{5}{32}$ at 16 lbs. The spring is painted with a red spot to ease identification.

Normal oil pressure is 30 p.s.i. minimum, and 80 p.s.i. maximum.

ENGINE REMOVAL.

This follows normal practice and the bonnet and radiator must be removed. The carburetters and air cleaners must also be taken off. The engine comes out of the car complete with the gearbox.

When disconnecting the auxiliaries and other items prior to engine removal note the reinforcement bracket from inside the propeller shaft tunnel. This must be removed.

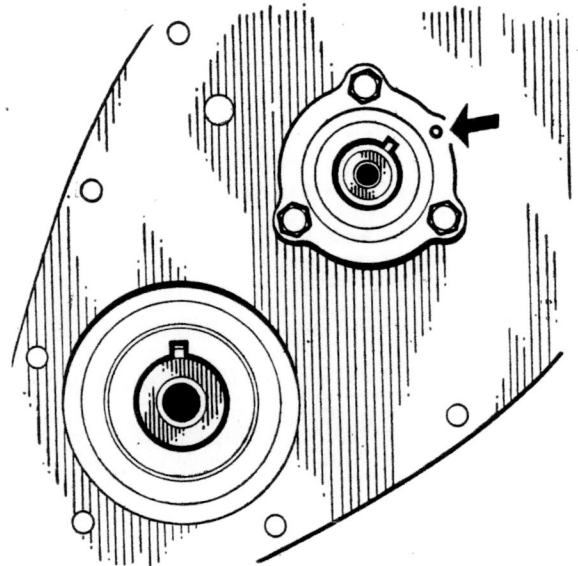

Fig. 4.—The notch in the pulley approaching the T.D.C. position for pistons 1 and 4. The inset shows the timing set at 5° before T.D.C.

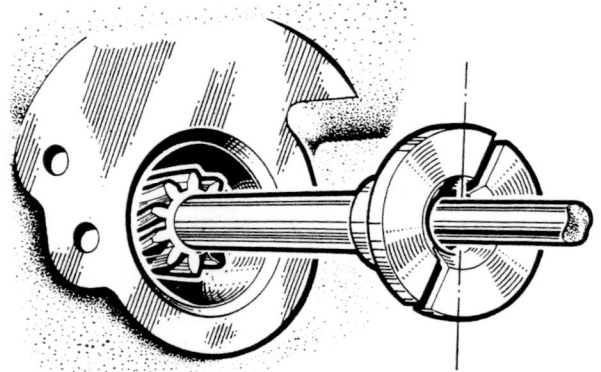

Fig. 6.—The arrow indicates the oil supply for the timing gear on early engines (see page 7). The crankshaft and camshaft wheel keys should be in the position shown when timing the engine.

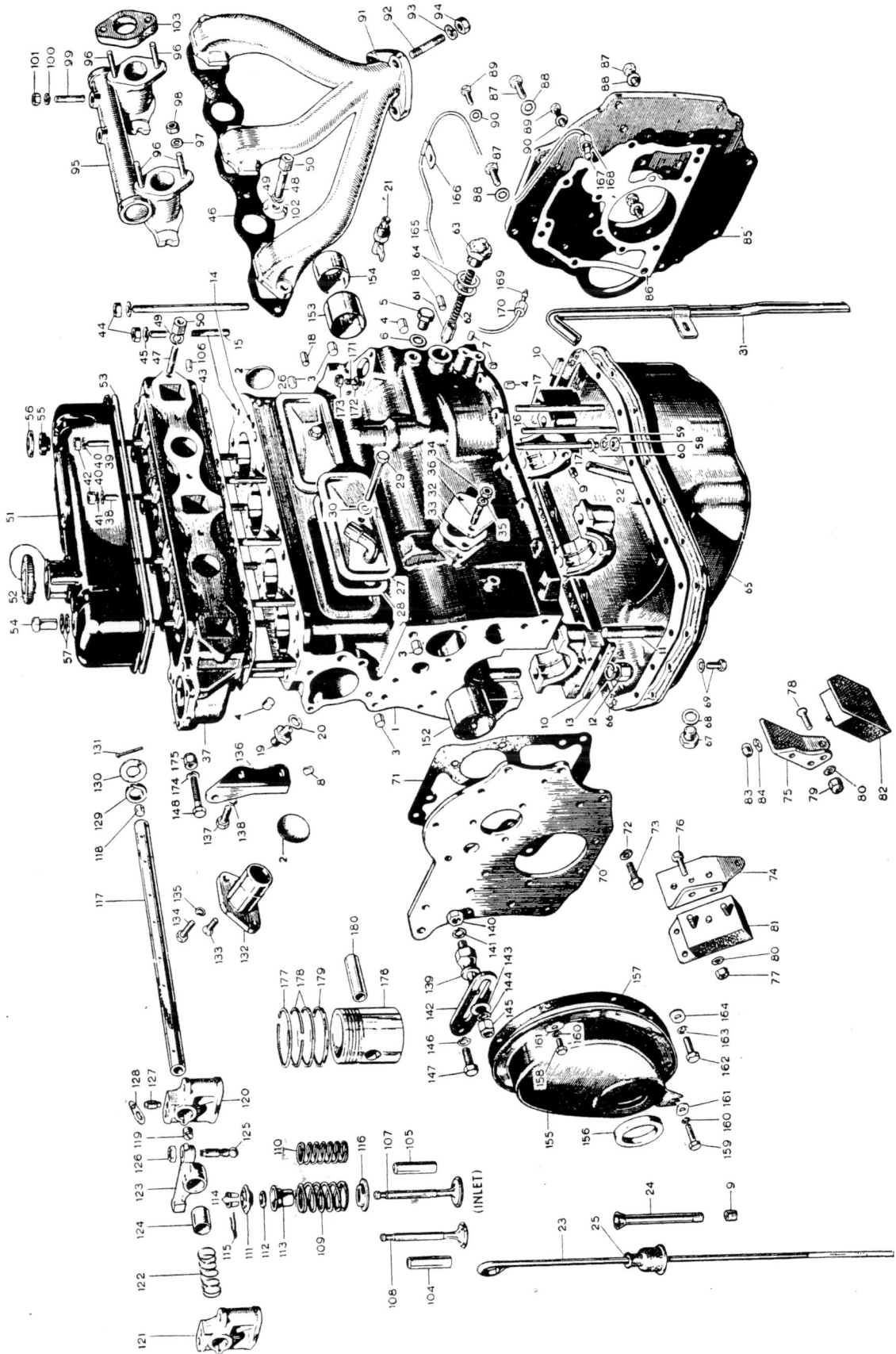

Fig. 7.—The engine compartment.

KEY TO FIGURE 7.

1—Block assembly—cylinder.
2—Plug—core hole.
3—Plug—oil gallery.
4—Plug—taper—crankcase oil hole.
5—Plug—screwed—transverse oil hole.
6—Washer—plug.
7—Plug—oil relief valve hole.
8—Plug—oil filter boss.
9—Plug—redundant dipper boss (and rear main bearing cap).
10—Joint—front/rear main bearing cap.
11—Stud—main bearing cap.
12—Nut—main bearing cap stud.
13—Washer—spring.
14—Stud (long) — cylinder head.
15—Stud (short) — cylinder head.
16—Stud (long) — oil pump.
17—Stud (short) — oil pump.
18—Dowel — gearbox mounting plate.
19—Union — oil gauge pipe.
20—Washer — union.
21—Tap — water drain.
22—Pipe—drain—rear bearing cap.
23—Dipper rod.
24—Tube—dipper rod.
25—Dust cap.
26—Cover—side—rear.
27—Cover—side—front—with elbow.
28—Joint—side covers.
29—Setscrew—covers.
30—Washer—setscrew.
31—Pipe—vent with clip—crankcase.
32—Plate—cylinder block blanking—N/S.
33—Joint—blanking plate.
34—Nut—blanking plate stud.
35—Washer—blanking plate stud.
36—Stud—L/H side crankcase blanking plate.
37—Cylinder head.
38—Stud—rocker bracket—short.
39—Stud—rocker bracket—long.
40—Washer—stud.
41—Washer—spring—stud.
42—Nuts—rocker bracket studs.
43—Joint—head to block.
44—Nut—cylinder head stud.
45—Washer—stud.

46—Joint—manifold to head.
47—Stud—exhaust manifold to head.
48—Stud—manifolds to head.
49—Washer—spring.
50—Nut—stainless steel.
51—Cover assembly—rocker gear.
52—Cap—oil filler and cable.
53—Joint—cover to head.
54—Cap nut—cover.
55—Bush—rubber—cap nut.
56—Cup washer—bush.
57—Washer—packing—cover stud.
58—Nut—oil pump stud.
59—Washer—spring.
60—Washer—plain.
61—Valve—oil release.
62—Spring—release valve.
63—Cap nut—release valve.
64—Washer—cap nut.
65—Reservoir—oil.
66—Joint—oil reservoir.
67—Plug—drain.
68—Washer—drain plug.
69—Setscrew—reservoir (with captive washer).
70—Plate—front mounting.
71—Joint—plate to block.
72—Spring washer.
73—Setscrew—plate to block.
74—Bracket—front R/H.
75—Bracket—front L/H.
76—Screw—R/H bracket to mounting plate.
77—Nut—R/H bracket to plate screw.
78—Screw—countersunk—L/H bracket to plate.
79—Nut—countersunk screw.
80—Washer—spring.
81—Mounting—R/H—front.
82—Mounting—L/H—front.
83—Washer—spring.
84—Nut—engine mounting to bracket.
85—Plate—gearbox mounting.
86—Joint—plate to block.
87—Setscrew—plate to block.
88—Lockwasher—setscrew.
89—Setscrew—plate to block.
90—Lockwasher—setscrew.

91—Manifold—exhaust.
92—Stud—exhaust pipe flange.
93—Washer.
94—Nut.
95—Manifold—induction.
96—Stud—carburetter.
97—Washer—plain.
98—Nut—carburetter stud.
99—Stud—inlet manifold (accelerator abutment bracket).
100—Spring washer.
101—Nut—inlet manifold stud.
102—Yoke—manifold.
103—Washer—carburetter insulating.
104—Guide—valve exhaust.
105—Guide—valve inlet.
106—Plug—oil hole.
107—Valve—inlet.
108—Valve—exhaust.
109—Spring—valve (outer).
110—Spring—valve (inner).
111—Cup—valve spring.
112—Packing ring—valve.
113—Shroud—valve guide.
114—Cotters—valve.
115—Circlip—cotter.
116—Collars—valve spring (bottom).
117—Shaft.
118—Plug—plain.
119—Plug—screwed.
120—Bracket—tapped hole.
121—Bracket—plain.
122—Spring—shaft—rocker spacing.
123—Rocker.
124—Bush.
125—Screw—tappet adjusting.
126—Locknut—screw.
127—Screw—shaft—locating.
128—Plate—locking—locating screw.
129—Washer—double coil.
130—Washer—plain.
131—Split pin.
132—Housing—distributor.
133—Screw—to block.
134—Screw—distributor to housing.

135—Washer—spring—screw.
136—Bracket—dynamo—rear.
137—Screw—bracket—to crankcase.
138—Spring washer.
139—Adjusting link pillar.
140—Nut—pillar to front plate.
141—Washer.
142—Adjusting link.
143—Washer—plain.
144—Washer—spring.
145—Nut—link to pillar.
146—Spring washer—link to dynamo.
147—Screw—link to dynamo.
148—Bolt—dynamo to bracket.
149—Plate—camshaft locating.
150—Screw—plate to back.
151—Washer—plate screw.
152—Liner—front camshaft bearing.
153—Liner—centre camshaft bearing.
154—Liner—rear camshaft bearing.
155—Cover complete—crankcase (front).
156—Felt ring.
157—Joint—crankcase front cover.
158—Setscrew—cover to engine plate.
159—Setscrew—cover and plate to bearing cap.
160—Washer—spring.
161—Washer—plain.
162—Setscrew—cover and plate to crankcase.
163—Washers—spring.
164—Washer—setscrew.
165—Pipe—ignition control.
166—Clip—pipe.
167—Nipple.
168—Nut—carburetter end.
169—Olive—distributor end.
170—Nut—distributor end.
171—Stud—tachometer pinion housing.
172—Washer—housing stud.
173—Nut—housing stud.
174—Washer—dynamo bolt.
175—Nut—dynamo bolt.
176—Piston assembly.
177—Ring—compression—1st.
178—Ring—compression—2nd and 3rd.
179—Ring—scraper.
180—Gudgeon pin.

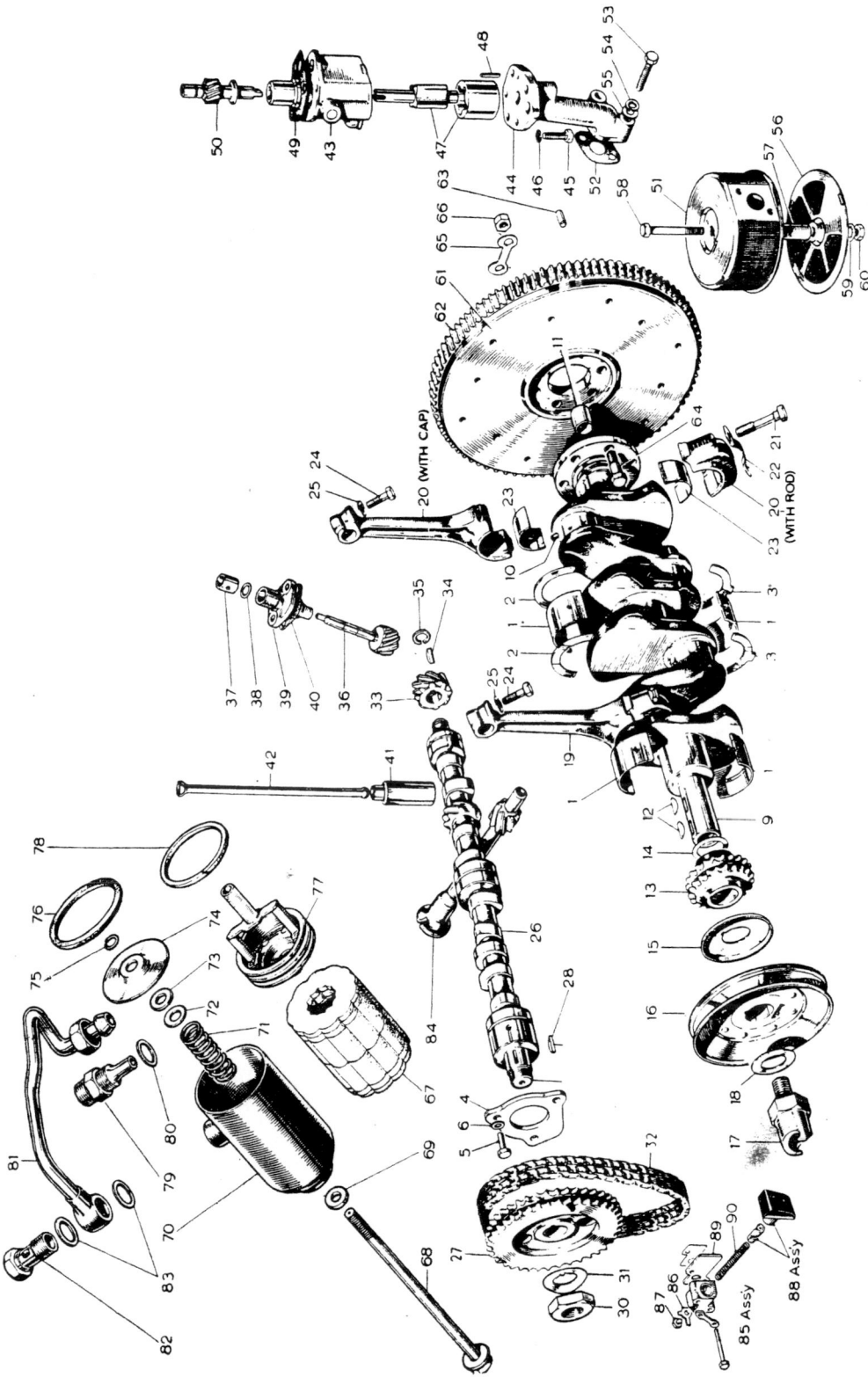

Fig. 8.—The camshaft, crankshaft and oil pump components.

1—Bearing—main—standard.
2—Thrust washer—upper.
3—Thrust washer—lower.
4—Plate—camshaft locating.
5—Screw—plate to engine.
6—Washer—spring—plate screw.
9—Crankshaft.
10—Restrictor—oil.
11—Bush—first motion shaft.
12—Key—gear—fan pulley.
13—Gear.
14—Washer—gear packing.
15—Oil thrower—front.
16—Pulley—crankshaft fan.
17—Nut—starting dog.
18—Lockwasher—nut.
19—Rod and cap—Nos. 1 and 3.
20—Rod and cap—Nos. 2 and 4.

21—Setscrew—cap.
22—Lockwasher.
23—Bearing—standard.
24—Screw—gudgeon pin clamp.
25—Spring washer—screw.
26—Camshaft.
27—Gear—camshaft.
28—Key—gear.
29—Tensioner ring—gear.
30—Nut—gear.
31—Lockwasher—nut.
32—Chain—camshaft timing.
33—Gear—tachometer drive.
34—Key—gear.
35—Spring ring.
36—Pinion—tachometer drive.
37—Oil seal—pinion.
38—Retaining ring.

39—Housing pinion.
40—Joint washer—housing.
41—Tappet—valve.
42—Pushrod.
43—Body and lug.
44—Cover.
45—Setscrew.
46—Spring washer.
47—Shaft driving—with rotors.
48—Dowels—cover.
49—Joint—pump to block.
50—Spindle—oil pump driving.
51—Body complete—oil strainer.
52—Joint—strainer to pump.
53—Setscrew—strainer to pump.
54—Spring washer.
55—Plain washer.

56—Cover—oil strainer.
57—Distance piece—cover.
58—Bolt—cover.
59—Washer—shakeproof.
60—Nut—cover bolt.
61—Flywheel.
62—Ring—starter.
63—Dowel—clutch.
64—Bolt—flywheel to crankshaft.
65—Lockwasher—bolt.
66—Nut—bolt.
67—Element—oil filter.
68—Bolt—centre.
69—Washer—sealing—small.
70—Container.
71—Spring.
72—Washer.

73—Washer—felt.
74—Pressure plate.
75—Circlip.
76—"O" ring.
77—Valve assembly.
78—Washer—sealing—large.
79—Adapter—oil filter connection.
80—Joint washer—pipe to crankcase.
81—Pipe assembly—filter to crankcase.
82—Screw—banjo union.
83—Washer—banjo union screw.
84—Spindle—distributor drive.
85—Tensioner—timing chain.
86—Lockwasher—plug.
87—Plug—body.
88—Slipper head and cylinder.
89—Backplate—body.
90—Spring.

21

OVERHAUL NOTES.

Use new oil seals round the valve stems at each overhaul. Fit the seals with the chamfered side down.

Soak the seals in oil before fitting.

When fitting new cam followers do so by selective assembly. The followers should just fall through their bores by their own weight.

There are packing washers behind the crankshaft gearwheel.

To check for correct thickness of washers use a straight edge placed across the two gear wheels and measure the gap with a feeler gauge. Subtract .005 from the gauge reading and add the resultant thickness of crankshaft gear packing washers.

Starting at engine number 259 a timing chain tensioner was fitted. On these engines the timing chain receives lubrication via the tensioner slipper and not as previously by an ejection of oil from the camshaft locating plate as shown in Fig. 5. The chain tensioner cannot be fitted easily to earlier engines.

The oil pressure relief valve is at the rear of the cylinder block on the left-hand side.

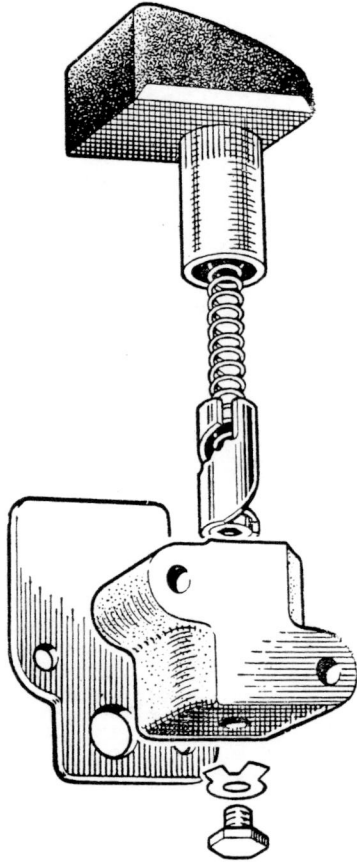

Fig. 9.—The chain tensioner components.

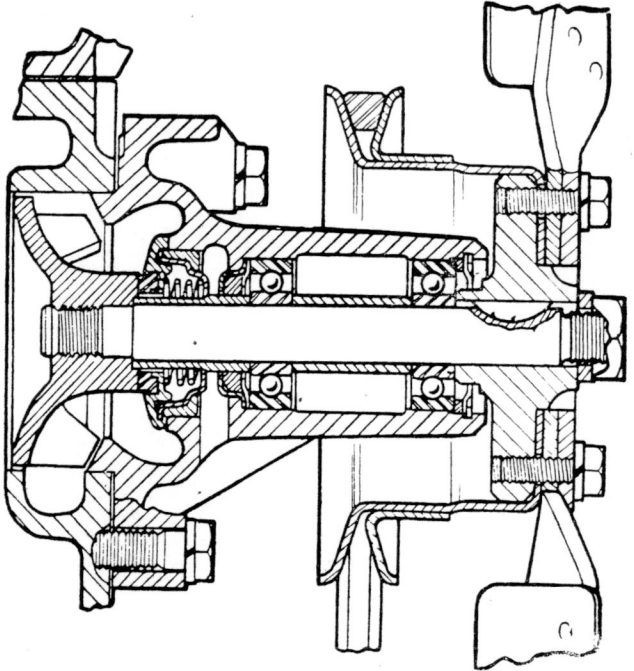

Fig. 10.—A section through the water pump showing the location of the components.

NOTE.—Later water pumps have a one piece bearing and shaft assembly.

GEARBOX

The gearbox cannot be removed with the engine in the chassis. To dismantle the gearbox take off the remote control assembly. Next, remove the extension from the gearbox, at the same time manoeuvring the remote control shaft selector lever from the selectors. Then take off the gearbox cover.

Note the overshoot stop.

Then take the shifter shafts from the box, noting the two dowels in the shift shaft locating block. Take care to catch the selector balls and springs. There are three of each.

Now take out the forks from the box in the following order, reverse, top and third and then first and second.

Then take off the gearbox front cover, noting shims between the cover and the bearing. It will then

be possible to tap out the layshaft and allow the gear cluster to fall to the bottom of the gearbox.

Further gearbox dismantling follows normal practice.

Dismantling of the third motion shaft follows normal practice and there is a third speed gear cone thrust washer plunger, which locks the washer in position.

When assembling the third motion shaft note that the longer brass bush is pushed up to the splines with the dog towards the front. This bush must be fitted so that the oil hole is in line with the one in the shaft, and the cut-away portion of the third speed splined bush will be over the locating peg hole when the dogs of the two bushes are engaged with the bush interlocking washer.

Fig. 11.—The gearbox components.

Further assembly is a reversal of the dismantling procedure.

At engine number 4525 the gearbox front end cover was modified. From that number the cover is fitted with an oil seal.

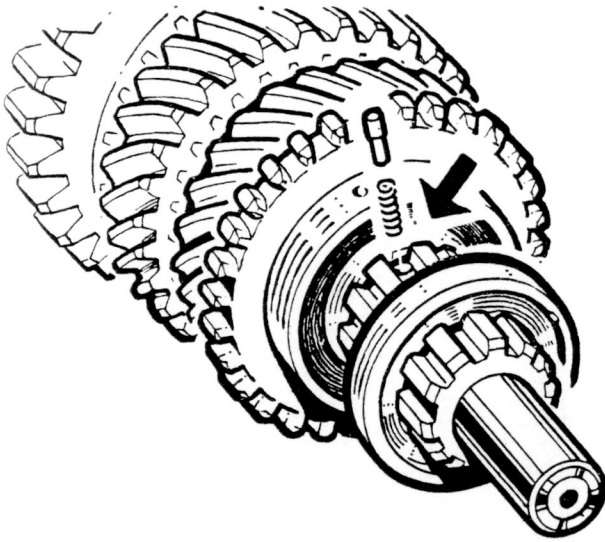

Fig. 12.—The arrow indicates the third speed thrust washer and locating peg. Note the hole in the gear cone.

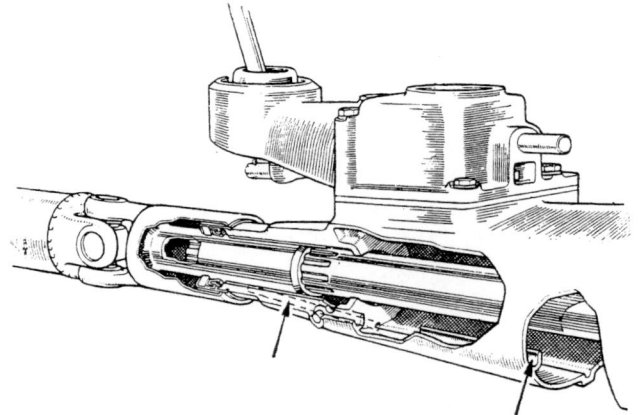

Fig. 13.—The sliding joint, showing the lubrication channels for the sliding joint bush.

KEY TO FIGURE 11:

1—Casing—gearbox.
2—Stud—front cover.
3—Plug—drain.
4—Dowel—side cover to gearbox.
5—Stud—gearbox extension.
6—Plug—blanking.
7—Joint washer—blanking plug.
8—Dust cover—clutch withdrawal lever.
9—Dipstick.
10—Felt.
11—Cover—front.
12—Joint—front cover.
13—Nut—front cover studs.
14—Spring washer—front cover stud.
15—Cover—side.
16—Joint—side cover.
17—Setscrew—side cover.
18—Spring washer—side cover screw.
19—Countersunk screw—side cover.
20—Shakeproof washer—countersunk screw.
21—Extension—gearbox.
22—Bush.
23—Oil seal.
24—Joint washer—oil seal.
25—Joint extension to gearbox.
26—Nut—gearbox extension stud.
27—Setscrew—gearbox extension.
28—Spring washer—stud and setscrew.
29—Plug—taper—gearbox extension.
30—Cover—extension side.
31—Joint—extension side cover.
32—Setscrew—extension side cover.
33—Spring washer.
34—Breather assembly.
35—Shaft—remote control.
36—Lever—selector—front.
37—Setscrew—front lever.
38—Spring washer—setscrew.

39—Key—selector lever.
40—Lever—selector—rear.
41—Bush—rear selector lever.
42—Circlip—lever bush.
43—Setscrew—rear lever.
44—Spring washer—setscrew.
45—Key—selector lever.
46—Fork—1st and 2nd speed.
47—Screw—fork locating.
48—Shaft—1st and 2nd speed fork.
49—Ball—shaft.
50—Spring—ball.
51—Fork—3rd and 4th speed.
52—Screw—fork locating.
53—Shaft—3rd and 4th speed fork.
54—Fork—reverse.
55—Screw—fork locating.
56—Shaft—reverse fork.
57—Block—shaft locating.
58—Setscrew—block to casing.
59—Spring washer—block screw.
60—Selector—1st and 2nd gear.
61—Screw—selector locating.
62—Selector—3rd and 4th gear.
63—Screw—selector locating.
64—Selector—reverse gear.
65—Screw—reverse gear selector.
66—Interlock arm complete.
67—Shaft—1st motion.
68—Nut—shaft.
69—Lockwasher.
70—Bearing—ball—shaft.
71—Spring ring—bearing.
72—Shim—bearing.
73—Rollers—needle—shaft.
74—Shaft—3rd motion.
75—Restrictor—oil.
76—Washer—thrust—front.
77—Washer—thrust—rear.
78—Peg—thrust washer—front.
79—Spring—peg.
80—Bearing—rear—3rd motion shaft
81—Housing—bearing.
82—Peg—locating.

83—Distance piece—speedometer gear.
84—Nut—shaft and speedometer gear.
85—Lockwasher.
86—Gear—speedometer drive.
87—Key—gear.
88—Pinion—speedometer drive.
89—Bush—pinion.
90—Oil seal—pinion.
91—Ring—oil seal retaining.
92—Joint—bush to rear cover.
93—Gear—1st speed.
94—Gear—2nd speed.
95—Synchroniser—2nd speed.
96—Ball—synchroniser.
97—Spring—ball.
98—Baulk ring—2nd speed gear.
99—Bush—2nd speed gear.
100—Gear—3rd speed.
101—Baulk ring—3rd and 4th gear.
102—Bush—3rd speed gear.
103—Ring—interlocking—2nd and 3rd bushes.
104—Coupling—sliding—3rd and 4th speed.
105—Synchroniser—3rd and 4th speed.
106—Ball—synchroniser.
107—Spring—ball.
108—Layshaft.
109—Gear unit—layshaft.
110—Bearing—needle roller—layshaft—outer.
111—Bearing—needle roller—layshaft—inner.
112—Spring ring—needle rollers.
113—Distance piece—bearing.
114—Washer—thrust—front.
115—Washer—thrust—rear.
116—Shaft—reverse.
117—Screw—locking—shaft.
118—Lockwasher—screw.
119—Gear—reverse.
120—Bush.

121—Bolt—gearbox to mounting plate.
122—Washer—spring.
123—Nut—mounting plate bolt.
124—Tower—remote control.
125—Dowel—remote control tower.
126—Core plug—tower.
127—Lever—change speed.
128—Knob—change speed lever.
129—Locknut—change speed lever knob.
130—Stop plate.
131—Snug—change speed ball.
132—Spring—change speed lever.
133—Cover—ball spring.
134—Circlip—ball spring cover.
135—Plunger—reverse selector.
136—Spring—reverse plunger.
137—Plug—reverse plunger.
138—Dowel—reverse plunger.
139—Ball—reverse plunger.
140—Spring—reverse plunger detent.
141—Gasket—control tower.
142—Bolt—short—tower.
143—Bolt—long—tower.
144—Spring washer.
145—Plug—ball retaining—box cover.
146—Washer—plug.
147—Plunger.
148—Spring—plunger.
149—Ball—selector lever.
150—Shaft—remote control.
151—Lever—front—selector.
152—Lever—rear—selector.
153—Setscrew—front and rear lever.
154—Spring washer.
155—Key.
156—Draught excluder—rubber—gear lever.
157—Ring—lever draught excluder.
158—Flexible bush—rear engine mounting.
159—Bolt—rear mounting bush.
160—Washer—spring.
161—Nut—rear mounting bush bolt.

P—(Int)

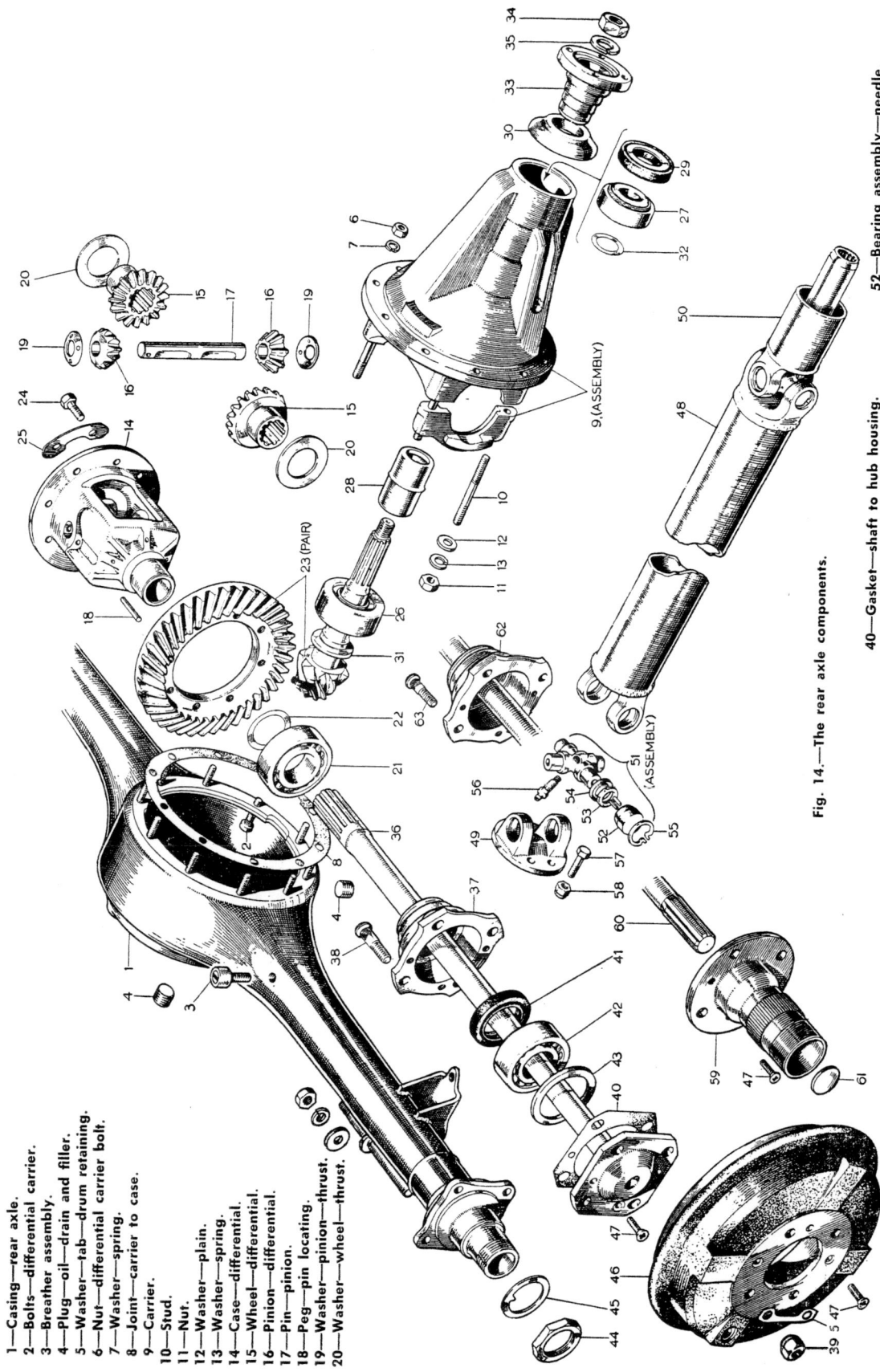

Fig. 14.—The rear axle components.

1—Casing—rear axle.
2—Bolts—differential carrier.
3—Breather assembly.
4—Plug—oil—drain and filler.
5—Washer—tab—drum retaining.
6—Nut—differential carrier bolt.
7—Washer—spring.
8—Joint—carrier to case.
9—Carrier.
10—Stud.
11—Nut.
12—Washer—plain.
13—Washer—spring.
14—Case differential.
15—Wheel—differential.
16—Pinion—differential.
17—Pin—pinion.
18—Peg—pin locating.
19—Washer—pinion—thrust.
20—Washer—wheel—thrust.

21—Bearing—differential.
22—Washer—packing—bearing (.002 inch).
23—Crownwheel and bevel pinion 10/43.
24—Bolt—crownwheel to case.
25—Bolt—lock—crownwheel bolt.
26—Bearing—bevel pinion—rear.
27—Bearing—bevel pinion—rear.
28—Spacer—bearing.
29—Oil seal—bearing—front.
30—Dust cover—oil seal.

31—Washer—bevel pinion (.112 inch).
32—Shim—front bevel pinion bearing (.004 inch).
33—Flange—universal joint.
34—Nut—flange.
35—Washer—spring—flange nut.
36—Shaft—rear axle. DW.
37—Hub assembly—rear. DW.
38—Stud—wheel. DW.
39—Nut—wheel stud. DW.

40—Gasket—shaft to hub housing.
41—Seal—oil—rear hub.
42—Bearing—rear hub.
43—Spacer—bearing. DW.
44—Locknut.
45—Washer—tab—locknut.
46—Drum—brake.
47—Screw—drum hub—axle shaft. DW.
48—Tubular shaft assembly.
49—Yoke—flange.
50—Yoke—sleeve assembly.
51—Journal and needle—kit set.

52—Bearing assembly—needle.
53—Gasket.
54—Retainer.
55—Circlip.
56—Lubricator—journal.
57—Bolt—shaft flange yoke—rear.
58—Nut—bolt.
59—Hub extension—R/H—rear. WW.
60—Shaft—axle. WW.
61—Welch plug—hub extension. WW.
DW — Disc Wheel.
WW — Wire Wheel.

25

REAR AXLE

The flanged axle half shafts are held in position by the wheel nuts and they are also located by two Phillips screws. When these parts have been removed the axle shaft may be pulled out.

The axle bearing assembly is held on the axle housing by means of a large nut. The hub needs a special puller to extract it. When reassembling it is essential that the outer face of the bearing spacer should protrude from .001 to .004 beyond the outer face of the hub and its paper washer when the bearing is pressed into position. This means that the bearing is gripped between the abutment shoulder in the hub and the driving flange of the axle shaft.

The differential bearings are marked with the word "thrust" and this is stamped on the thrust face of each bearing.

Note also that shims are fitted between the inner ring of each bearing and the differential case.

Crownwheel bearing housing nuts tightening torque 45 lbs. ft. Crownwheel run-out .002.

In common with other B.M.C. rear axles the setting of the crownwheel and pinion is done by means of a clock gauge and special tools and it is not possible to set the axle without them.

Pinion bearing pre-load 11 to 13 lbs. in. without the oil seal, 14 to 16 lbs. in. with the oil seal.

Crownwheel bearing pinch is .002 each side.

Tighten the driving flange nut to 140 lbs. ft.

For further information see "Nuffield Rear Axles" in the Service Section.

STEERING

This is the M.G. rack and pinion type and in all major respects is the same as the M.G. "TF" steering described in that section of this manual.

The steering column is universally jointed and due to this fact it is extremely important that the column be correctly aligned.

For the universal joint to be completely unloaded the centre line of the steering column and the centre line of the steering rack pinion must pass through the centre of the universal joint spider when the assembly is viewed from above, and from the side. Failure to ensure complete freedom at the universal joint will load the steering pinion upper bearing and

cause extreme wear and stiffness in the steering. See Fig. 15.

The steering gearbox is held on brackets with shims to ensure correct alignment. When the shims have been determined they are riveted in position to prevent their loss.

To make quite sure that the steering geometry is correct it is important that the tie-rods are adjusted to exactly equal lengths. This can be checked by measuring from the end of the flat to the locknut on each side.

When adjusting, also make quite sure that the machined undersides of the ball joints are in the same plane.

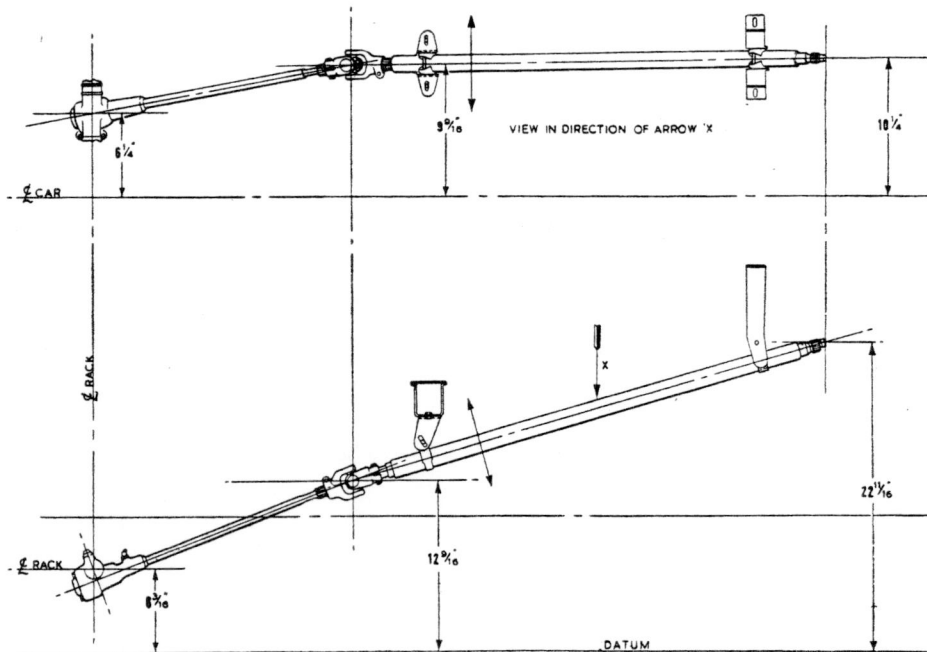

Fig. 15.—Steering column alignment.

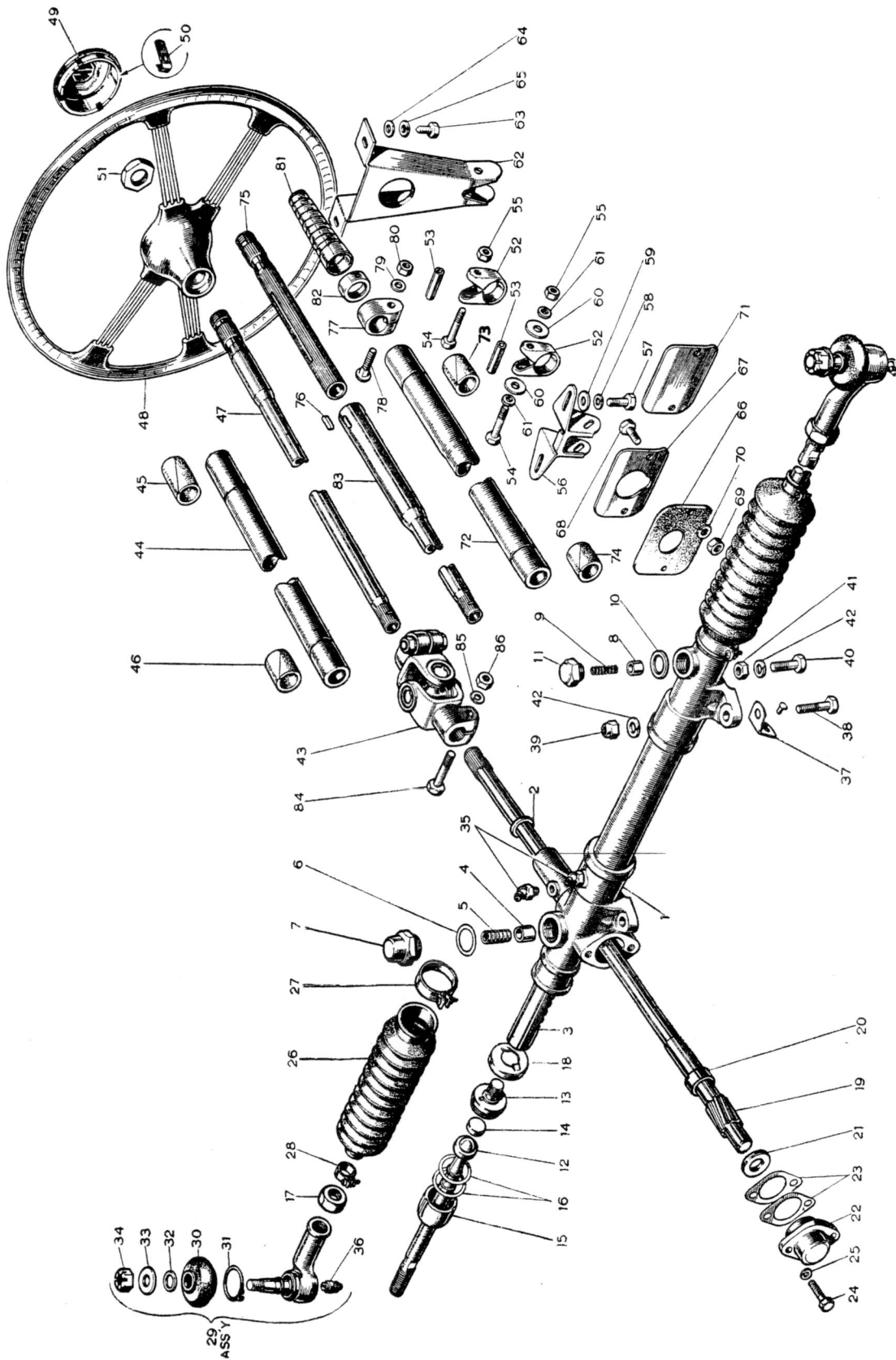

Fig. 16.—The steering gear components.

KEY TO FIGURE 16:

1—Housing assembly—rack.
2—Seal—pinion shaft.
3—Rack—steering.
4—Pad—rack damper.
5—Spring—rack damper.
6—Shim—pad housing.
7—Housing—rack damper.
8—Pad—rack damper secondary.
9—Spring—rack damper secondary.
10—Washer—rack damper secondary.
11—Housing—rack damper secondary.
12—Rod—tie.
13—Housing—male ball.
14—Seat—ball.
15—Housing—female ball.
16—Shim—ball housing—.003 inch.
17—Locknut—tie-rod.
18—Lockwasher—tie-rod.
19—Pinion—steering.
20—Washer—thrust—upper pinion.
21—Washer—thrust—lower pinion.
22—Bearing—pinion tail.
23—Shim .005 inch—tail bearing.
24—Screw—bearing to steering box.
25—Washer—spring—bearing screw.
26—Seal—rack.
27—Clip assembly—large—seal.
28—Clip assembly—small—seal.
29—Socket assembly—ball.

30—Boot—rubber.
31—Clip—boot.
32—Ring—boot clip.
33—Washer—ball socket.
34—Nut—ball socket.
35—Greaser—pinion/rack.
36—Greaser—ball socket.
37—Shim—steering rack to brackets.
38—Bolt—rack to bracket (front).
39—Nut—rack to bracket (nyloc).
40—Bolt—rack to bracket (rear).
41—Nut—rack to bracket (rear).
42—Washer—spring—rack to bracket.
43—Universal joint—steering column.
44—Tube—outer.
45—Bush—felt—upper end.
46—Bush—felt—lower end.
47—Tube assembly—inner.
48—Wheel—steering.
49—Cover—steering wheel.
50—Spring clip—cover.
51—Nut—steering wheel.
52—Clamp—steering column.
53—Distance piece—clamp.
54—Bolt—clamp.
55—Nut—clamp bolt.
56—Bracket (lower)—steering column.
57—Screw—bracket to frame.
58—Washer—spring—bracket to frame.

59—Washer—plain—bracket to frame.
60—Washer—plain—lower bracket to clamp.
61—Washer—spring—lower bracket to clamp.
62—Bracket—upper—steering column.
63—Screw—bracket to body rail.
64—Washer—plain.
65—Washer—spring.
66—Seal—rubber—column.
67—Retainer—column seal.
68—Screw—seal and retainer to dash.
69—Nut—seal/retainer screw.
70—Washer—spring—seal/retainer screw.
71—Blanking plate.
72—*Tube—column outer.
73—*Bush—upper.
74—*Bush—lower.
75—*Top end—adjustable.
76—*Key—top end.
77—*Clamp—rollar.
78—*Bolt—clamp.
79—*Washer—spring—clamp bolt.
80—*Nut—clamp bolt.
81—*Spring cover.
82—*Cup—spring cover.
83—*Tube assembly—inner.
84—Bolt—universal joint.
85—Washer—spring.
86—Nut—universal joint bolt.
*Optional equipment.

FRONT SUSPENSION

Up to Car No. 15151. Spring free height 9.28 $\pm\frac{1}{16}$. Static laden length 6.60 $\pm\frac{1}{32}$. Static laden length at load of 1095 lbs. Maximum deflection 4 inches.

From Car No. 15152. Spring free height 8.88 $\pm\frac{1}{16}$. Static laden length 6.60 $\pm\frac{1}{32}$. Load at static laden length 1095 lbs. ±20 lbs.

For dismantling details refer to the M.G. "TF" section in this manual, for the two suspensions are very similar in general construction.

Camber angle 1° positive to $\frac{1}{2}$° negative on full bump. Castor angle 4°. King pin inclination 9° to $10\frac{1}{2}$° on full bump. There is no toe-in, the wheels being set parallel.

BRAKES

Lockheed hydraulic with two leading shoes at the front. Drum diameter 10 inches, width $1\frac{3}{4}$ inches. Lining dimensions 9.6 inches long x $1\frac{3}{4}$ inches wide. Material is Ferodo DM12.

The brake pedal pad must be depressed $\frac{1}{2}$ inch before the piston in the master cylinder begins to move.

CLUTCH

Borg. & Beck A6G, single dry plate, 8 inches in diameter. Facing material is Borglite.

Pressure springs are black and yellow, whilst the damper springs are white with light green stripes.

Clearance between the master cylinder pushrod and the piston is $\frac{1}{32}$. This will give the correct free movement at the clutch pedal pad.

ELECTRICAL

STARTER.

Lucas M35G. Brush spring tension 30 to 40 ounces.

GENERATOR.

C39PV2.
Two Lucas 6 volt batteries, SG9E, are fitted.
Coil LA1210. Control box RB106/2.

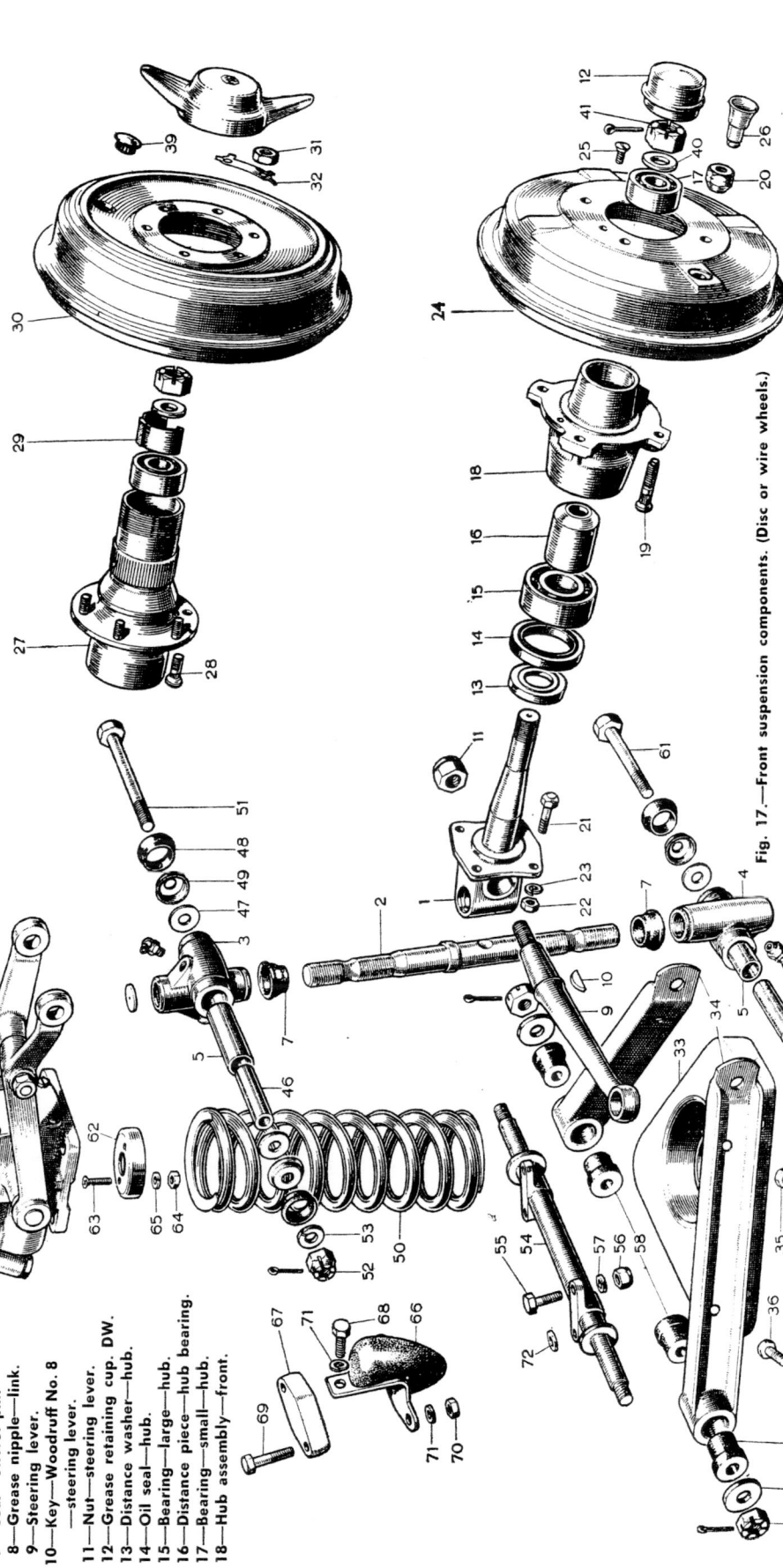

Fig. 17.—Front suspension components. (Disc or wire wheels.)

1—Steering knuckle—L/H.
2—Swivel pin—L/H.
3—Link—swivel pin—upper L/H.
4—Link—swivel pin—lower L/H.
5—Bush.
6—Plate.
7—Seal—swivel pin.
8—Grease nipple—link.
9—Steering lever.
10—Key—Woodruff No. 8—steering lever.
11—Nut—steering lever.
12—Grease retaining cup. DW.
13—Distance washer—hub.
14—Oil seal—hub.
15—Bearing—large—hub.
16—Distance piece—hub bearing.
17—Bearing—small—hub.
18—Hub assembly—front.

19—Stud—wheel. DW.
20—Nut—wheel stud. DW.
21—Bolt—brake backplate.
22—Nut—backplate bolt.
23—Washer—spring—backplate bolt.
24—Drum—brake. DW.

25—Screw—countersunk—drum to hub. DW.
26—Plug—large—brake drum. DW.
27—Hub assembly—front L/H. WW.
28—Stud. WW.
29—Grease retainer. WW.
30—Drum—brake. WW.

31—Nut—drum to hub. WW.
32—Locking tab—drum to hub. WW.
33—Spring pan assembly.
34—Bottom wishbone assembly.
35—Screw—spring pan to wishbone.
36—Screw—spring pan to wishbone.

37—Nut—spring pan to wishbone screw.
38—Washer—spring—pan to wishbone screw.
39—Plug—brake drum—large. WW.
40—Washer.
41—Nut—L/H thread.
42—Hydraulic damper.
43—Stud—hydraulic damper to crossmember.

44—Nut—hydraulic damper to crossmember stud.
45—Washer—spring—hydraulic damper to crossmember.
46—Distance tube—link.
47—Thrust washer—link.
48—Seal—link.
49—Support—link seal.

50—Spring—coil.
51—Bolt—wishbone to link.
52—Nut—castle—wishbone to link.
53—Washer—spring—wishbone to link.
54—Wishbone pivot.
55—Bolt—pivot to member.
56—Nut—pivot to member bolt.
57—Washer—spring—pivot to member bolt.
58—Bush—bottom wishbone.
59—Washer—wishbone pivot.
60—Nut—slotted—wishbone pivot.
61—Bolt—bottom wishbone to link.
62—Spigot—spring.

63—Screw—spigot to member.
64—Nut—spigot to member screw.
65—Washer—spigot to member screw.
66—Check rubber.
67—Distance piece—check rubber.
68—Screw—check rubber to member.
69—Bolt—check rubber to member.
70—Nut—check rubber to member—bolt.
71—Washer—spring—check rubber to member.
72—Washer—plain—under front outer head pivot to member bolt.
DW—Disc wheel.   WW—Wire wheel.

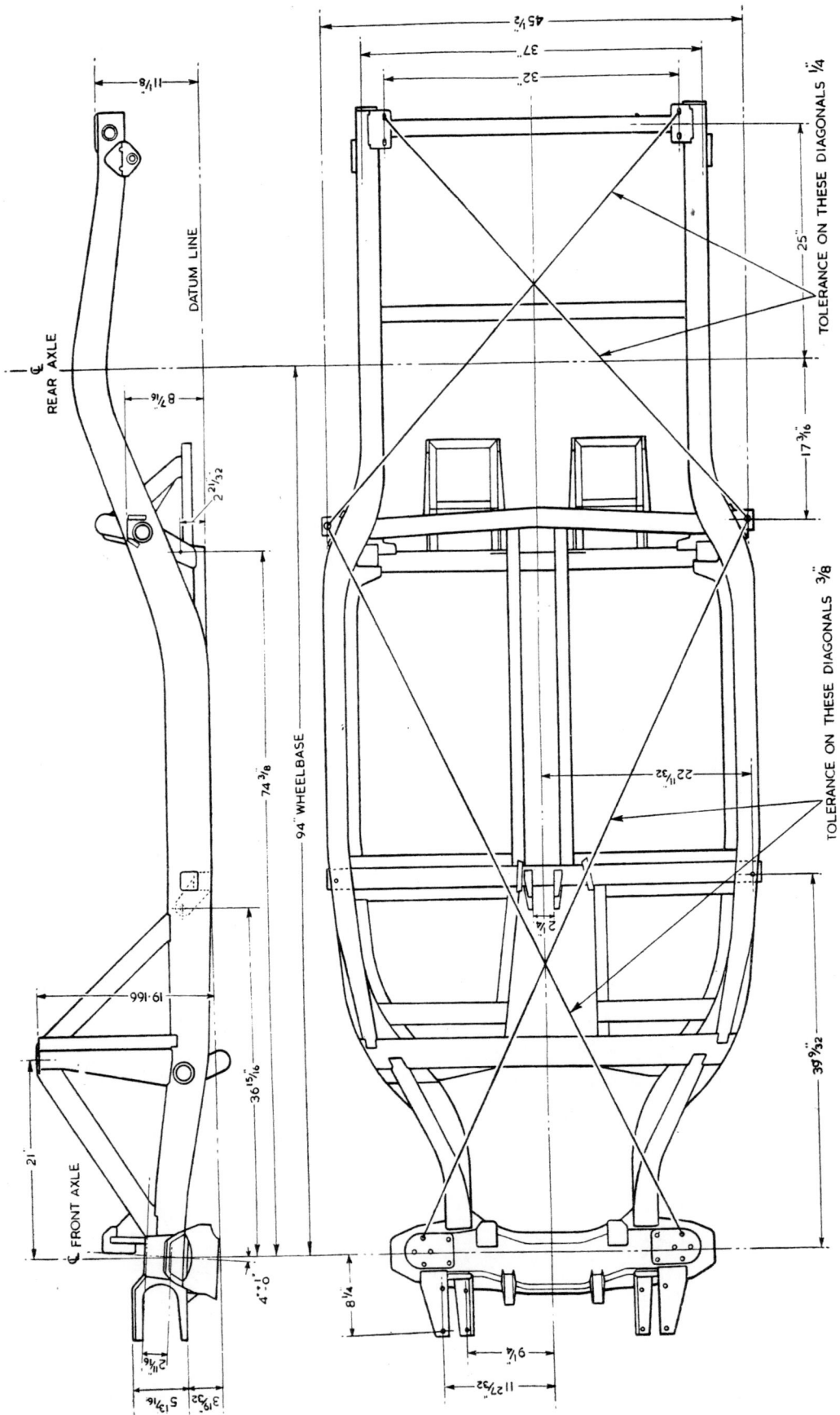

Fig. 18.—Chassis checking points.

TOLERANCE ON THESE DIAGONALS ¼

TOLERANCE ON THESE DIAGONALS ⅜

45½

37

32

25"

17 ³⁄₁₆

22 ¹¹⁄₃₂

39 ⁹⁄₃₂

2 ¼

11 ²⁷⁄₃₂

6 ¹⁄₄

8 ¼

DATUM LINE

REAR AXLE

11 ⅛

8 ⅝

2 ²¹⁄₃₂

74 ³⁄₈

94" WHEELBASE

16·199

36 ¹⁵⁄₁₆

21

FRONT AXLE

4·· 1"·0

2 ¹¹⁄₁₆

3 ⁹⁄₃₂

5 ¹³⁄₁₆

ROAD TEST 3/Apr/62

MGA 1600

Potent power pack: the 1600 cc engine gives the MGA notable get-up-and-go

ALTHOUGH it is some years since we last tested the MGA no great changes have been effected in this very robust, very likeable and very popular sports car. But certain alterations were made to the car in June of last year including the increase in engine size from 1588 cc to the present 1622 cc. New grille and lamp treatments, as well as some detail refinments, distinguished the new version, which was designated the Mark 2.

No concessions have been made to the add-a-little-chrome brigade in revising the car, but the familiar grille is slightly altered

Even with these changes the car had a familiarity which was undeniably pleasing. So much has been written about the best loved name in current British sports cars that it is superfluous to go into great detail about a model so well tried and so well refined over the years. It is worthwhile, nevertheless, to recall some of the detail changes which have resulted in a good car becoming an excellent one.

The increase capacity was achieved by an increase in bore dimension from 75.4 mm to 76.2. In conjunction with this, inlet and exhaust valves were increased in diameter, and the ports were altered to improve gas flow. In keeping with the better fuels now available an 8.9 to 1 compression ratio is fitted as standard, although the old 8.3 to 1 can be obtained for markets were 100 octane fuel is not readily available. The net result of these engine modifications has been to raise bhp from 80 at 5,500 revs to 90 at 5,200, and to get a similar ten per cent improvement in torque albeit on a slightly sharper curve. With the increase in power thus gained it has been possible to raise the final drive ratio from 4.3 to 1 to 4.1 to 1 giving 17.7 mph per 1,000 revs in top gear as against the 17 mph previously. Interior trim has been improved, notably by covering the dashboard in leathercloth, but controls and instrumentation have been left unaltered.

The car tested had Lockheed brakes on all four wheels, disc at the front and drum at the rear, and a soft top. Removable and fixed hard tops are available.

Since the main improvements to the car have been in the field of engine performance it was natural that we should look in our test to the acceleration and maximum speed of the Mark 2 for comparison with its predecessor. Overall the comparison had to be adjudged disappointing, for the improvement in acceleration and maximum speed is no more than marginal, although the higher rear axle ratio allows for greater speeds in the intermediate gears. However, there was a noteworthy improvement in low speed pulling power and also in the comfort of high cruising speeds between 70 and 90 mph. In this context, of course, it must be remembered that the MG was a very lively little car before. It remains so, even if the performance figures can be bettered in this day by a number of cars with considerably less engine capacity and more carrying room.

Anybody trying the MGA for the first time will be immediately impressed by that feeling of robustness which only comes to a car which has been developed over a period of years. Contributing to this feeling in the MGA is the very solid tubular chassis frame and the strong, curvacious steel body shell which seems to discourage all forms of squeaks and rattles. After driving a number of cars more modern in conception and more advanced in styling we readily appreciated the feeling of solidity and longevity which the MGA imparts.

Handling is excellent in a slightly pre-war manner. Spring movements are short and frequencies high. The dampers really do their work. Yet despite the firm ride the car is never uncomfortable except on really execrable surfaces. For the most part, on British roads, the firm springing is a real joy because it means the car can be cornered on main roads at high speed without roll or and appearance of being "on the ragged edge". Steering is high geared and precise, although perhaps a little heavy at low speeds, the gearbox is extremely positive, and the Lockheed brakes, discs at the front and drums at the rear, are really excellent, requiring a fair amount

Getting in and out is as difficult as it has been with most of the MG line. Tight skirts not advised for the lady friends!

Hood on the way up looks slightly dishevelled (so were the putter-uppers!) but once up (below) all is snug and serene

Spare wheel impinges tragically on boot space, but if you are prepared to leave it at home two suitcases would go in

parcels is indeed one of the weakest points of the MGA, for the best part of the boot is occupied by the 15 in. spare wheel to such good purpose that a small suitcase and a squashy bag would be the limit of touring luggage that could be carried. All is businesslike under the bonnet although accessibility is not of the highest order.

The car behaved faultlessly throughout our test with one exception. The makers had adjured us to use 100 octane fuel only, but on one occasion it was not possible to obtain this. Ordinary super petrol was used and thereafter the engine invariably ran on when the ignition had been switched off, sometimes for quite a number of revolutions. Even when the 100 octane fuel was used again this fault did not entirely disappear.

In short we found the Mark 2 MGA to be a logical if not very large improvement over the earlier model, and frankly we found *that* a sufficiently enjoyable motorcar to be wholeheartedly glad that the present model retains such a large proportion of its character. No doubt the time is not very far distant when the MGA will be redesigned completely. Until that moment comes the enthusiast has in this car a vehicle of traditional sporting appeal, thoroughly well matured and as strong as a battleship.

of pedal effort but giving ultra-rapid deceleration from any speed. There is still a touch of character about the interior of the MGA. There is the familiar horn button in the centre of the dashboard, which always takes at least a couple of days to get used to; there is the usual multitude of knobs and dials, the wire cable door pulls, the fly-off handbrake, and the most pleasant four-spoke steering wheel with spokes set at ten to two and twenty to four.

Although the weather was cold for most of our test we could not resist putting the hood down and enjoying some open-air motoring which is the real pleasure of a car like the MG. With the hood down in winter it is certainly a pretty spartan driving position, but the substantial sidescreens now provided can limit the draught to a steady breeze from behind which a turned-up coat collar effectively screens. When the hood is erect large quarter panels in the rear give nearly perfect all-round visibility. The MG has never conceded anything to the easy-to-put-up-hood brigade, and, true to the tradition, this model requires some good hard work from two people to get the hood erected. We never entirely solved the purpose of a drape which covered over the hood when it was folded away, and which contained pockets. Certainly there is not sufficient room for anything more than a flat briefcase to be stowed behind the seats when the hood is down. Accommodation for luggage and

SPECIFICATION :

ENGINE:
Four cylinders; bore 76·2 mm (3·0 in), stroke 88·9 mm (3·5 in). Cubic capacity, 1622 cc. Compression ratio, 8·9 to 1. Overhead valves, operated by pushrods and rockers. Maximum bhp, 90 at 5,500 rpm. Torque, 97 lb ft at 4,000 rpm. Twin SU carburettors; fuel tank capacity, 10 gals. Electrical system: 12V —two 6V 58 amp/h batteries.

TRANSMISSION:
Single dry plate clutch. Four speed gearbox with synchromesh on top three ratios. Overall gear ratios: 1st, 14·9; 2nd, 9·08; 3rd, 5·63; top, 4·1 to 1. Central remote control gear lever.

CHASSIS:
Suspension: front, independent by wishbones and coil springs rear, live axle, semi-elliptic leaf springs. Lever-type dampers front and rear. Lockheed hydraulic brakes, discs at front and drums at rear. Four-spoke steering wheel; turns lock to lock, 2·6. Tyre size: 5·60-15in.

DIMENSIONS:

			ft	in
Wheelbase	...	...	7	10
Track: front	...	...	3	11½
Track: rear	...	...	4	0¾
Overall length	...	...	13	0
Overall width	...	...	4	10
Overall height	...	...	4	2
Ground clearance	...	...		6
Turning circle	...	...	31	1
Kerb weight	...	...	18 cwt.	

PERFORMANCE:
Acceleration through gears:

mph	sec
0-30	4·1
0-40	5·9
0-50	8·5
0-60	12·8
0-70	17·4
0-80	23·4
0-90	35·0

(Weather fine, dry, cold for testing)

Speeds in gears (approximate maxima during testing):

1st	30 mph
2nd	50 mph
3rd	80 mph
4th	100 mph

Speedometer correction: 6% fast at 100 mph.

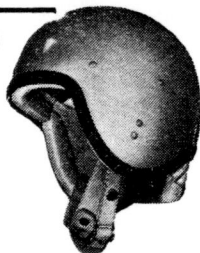

M.G. A Coupé

Derived from the successful open model, the coupé has attractions of its own

MENTION the term "sports car" to the average motorist, and nine times out of ten he will immediately think of a small open two-seater with generally angular lines and a near-vertical radiator bearing n octagonal badge. For it is no exaggeration to say that the M.G. is probably the most familiar of sports cars throughout the world. It has always been produced in fairly substantial numbers, and there has never been any doubt about how substantial it is as a car. Proof of this is provided daily by the sight of examples of almost every model since the M-type among the traffic on our roads.

The A-type coupé which is the subject of this touring trial is as yet a comparative stranger in Britain. The bulk of M.G. production being exported to America, comparatively few reach British enthusiasts' hands, and the coupé version in particular is a rarity. Further, being a closed car—although still a two-seater—and having pleasant, curvaceous lines, it does not perhaps represent the average motorist's conception of a sports car as previously defined. But to the enthusiastic motorist, the A-type coupé is precisely right; it is a fast, good looking, economical, well finished, safe vehicle. In fact, a sports car.

Both the coupé and the open two-seater versions of the M.G. A are based on a rigid chassis with box-section side members outswept amidships to enable the occupants to sit within the frame instead of on top of it. A tubular scuttle structure, supported by box-section bracing members provides the front end of the frame with stiffness in depth, while at the rear where the frame is upswept to pass over the rear axle, stiffness is increased by a fixed bulkhead and by box-section cross members. The all steel body with its deeply drawn steel roof undoubtedly contributes to the high all-round rigidity of the structure.

The benefit is seen not only in the very high standards of roadworthiness, but also in smaller details such as the freedom from drumming and vibration and the silence of the windows and doors, even when the car is rushed over

places where signs are displayed saying "Road Works" at speeds in the high 70's. Usually the price paid for such freedom from the effects of external conditions is high weight. The M.G. A coupé weighs 18 cwt. 3 qrs., which may seem high for a 1½-litre car; but not when the evident quality of the body and its trimming is taken into account.

Superficially, the coupé is entirely in the modern styling idiom. The windscreen is well wrapped round the sides of the passenger accommodation, and the rear window, in three sections, comes right round to provide a bright interior and exceptional all round visibility. Yet in some ways the car is old-fashioned. Although the tail is long, the bonnet is even longer, because of course, much of the rearward part of the nose covers the occupants' leg room. The driver thus looks along an aristocratically long nose, which curves away to give good visibility close to the front of the car.

Underneath the bonnet is the B.M.C. B-series engine in its most highly tuned production form. The 1,489 c.c. unit produces 72 b.h.p. at 5,500 r.p.m. on a compression ratio of 8.3 : 1. The two inclined S.U. 1½-in. carburetters have deep air cleaners, which are placed well out of the way, so that accessibility under the bonnet is quite good. The dip-stick is not easy to reach, and the Tecalemit oil filter would probably be best changed from beneath the car.

As in every production M.G., the engine is surprisingly flexible. At town speeds, moreover, it is remarkably quiet, and only at maximum speed does one become aware of a small engine doing a tremendous amount of work. Just how tremendous may be gauged from the acceleration and maximum speed figures recorded. The best speed recorded in top gear was 105 m.p.h., and the coupé frequently recorded 101-102 m.p.h. The speedometer was 4 per cent fast at 60 m.p.h. and 6 per cent fast at 100 m.p.h.

Third gear maximum, at the recommended engine speed limit of 5,500 r.p.m., was 74 m.p.h. and second gear maximum was 45 m.p.h. Top gear (4.3 : 1) will carry the coupé up a gradient of 1 in 10, third gear suffices for 1 in 7, while second can cope easily with 1 in 4½. Accelerating from rest, starting in bottom gear, the M.G. A reaches 30 m.p.h. in 4.5 sec., 40 m.p.h. in 7.2 sec., and 50 m.p.h. in 10.8 sec. Another 4.5 sec. with the throttle held flat and 60 m.p.h. is recorded, while only 22 sec., are needed to reach 70 m.p.h. from rest. Intermediate acceleration figures are as follows:

			2nd sec.	3rd sec.	Top sec.
20–40	..	..	4.1	6.1	10.1
30–50	..	..	–	7.2	11.0
40–60	..	..	–	7.8	10.4
50–70	..	..	–	8.7	11.5
60–80	..	..	–	–	16.6

The four-speed gearbox with synchromesh on second, third and top, is a delight to use, of course, although several near-criticisms can be made. First, although the lever is short and firm and well located in the centre of the floor, it might be improved by the addition of possibly an inch to its overall length. At the moment sufficient effort is needed in making a rapid change, to cause the palm of the hand to become sensitive after a few hurried mountain miles. A slightly longer lever might reduce the effort required. Secondly, the high maximum speed of the car makes one wish occasionally for a slightly closer third gear, because there is a long gap between 105 m.p.h. and the maximum speed in third, and the ability to engage third earlier without rushing the needle of the rev counter right off the clock would occasionally be reassuring. Thirdly, synchromesh on bottom gear would be a tremendous help, not because bottom gear is difficult to engage at any time, but again, because it would be so reassuring to be able to drop quickly into first without any delay while the driver brushes up his engine/road speed co-ordinating experience. It was felt that this item would have a particular attraction on the American market where the model is so popular, particularly because it is essential to start in first gear. You can start in second, but some care with the fairly heavy clutch pedal is needed to avoid stalling the engine.

One notable feature of the car was that even after prolonged running with the rev counter needle exceeding

5,000 r.p.m. (equivalent to 85 m.p.h. in top gear) the engine remains unruffled. It also provides an acceptable degree of economy. Overall fuel consumption for some 430 miles was 33.4 m.p.g. Short runs and prolonged use of high engine speeds reduced this figure to 27.8 m.p.g. over the next 300 miles, but the driver who is not in a hurry can expect over 30 m.p.g. constantly. The fuel tank has a capacity of 10 gallons, which is comforting on long runs.

High average speeds can be recorded without the slightest effort. On one occasion the car was driven from west of Aylesbury over busy trunk roads and quiet country lanes into the inner suburbs of London at an average speed of just over 53 m.p.h. On another occasion it averaged 51 m.p.h. from the end of the Watford by-pass into Fleet Street. On main road journeys such averages are standard practice.

(ABOVE) *The interior of the coupé is exceptionally well trimmed and equipped, and is comfortable over long periods* (TOP, RIGHT) *Although not particularly tidy, the engine compartment is reasonably accessible*

(RIGHT) *Disc wheels were fitted on the car used for photography purposes, but the car used for performance tests had wire wheels with centre lock hubs. In either form the car is aesthetically pleasing*

Windscreen and rear window are wrapped well round for good visibility and the bumpers protect the four corners of the car. Ventilation, with wind down windows and swivelling quarter lights can be carefully controlled

Travelling at such speeds causes no discomfort to driver or passenger and apart from the fatigue caused by the need to concentrate, leaves the driver physically untired. The two front bucket seats are well shaped and exceptionally well trimmed. They support the back and secure the occupant against side-ways "G". They might however be a fraction higher off the floor. As it is the nearside wing is seen with difficulty by a driver under 6 ft., and in any event the rear view mirror is occasionally a hindrance to vision on that side

The coil spring and wishbone front suspension and semi-elliptic rear suspension do their work effectively. Bumps are absorbed without undue effect, and although the ride is a little hard at low speeds on poor surfaces, the Armstrong hydraulic dampers do their work well. There is practically no roll and the M.G. can really be flung at sharp corners without a great deal of juggling with throttle and steering wheel.

The rack and pinion steering is a model of its type, and the general responsiveness of the car a delight to the driver. With only 2¾ turns from lock to lock, the car can be turned inside 30 ft. The car understeers slightly, and achieves a high standard of handling. There is no lost motion in the steering system of course, and it feels as if response is as quick as thought itself. Even in the wet it was found that the car had no vices. Cross-winds encountered during the tests also failed to affect the car.

Similarly, the brakes are admirable. The 10-in. Lockheed brakes never became hot, and did not fade, even after a deliberate attempt was made to upset them. The knock-off wire wheels no doubt play their part in this result, while the 5.60 x 15 Road Speed tyres on the two cars played their part too, in achieving a maximum deceleration of 96 per cent according to the Tapley meter. The fly-off hand brake though pleasant in action, and efficient, was awkwardly placed, and a short driver found that it was difficult to release it when the seat was well forward. Even a tall driver had difficulty when wearing gloves, because he could not get his fingers round the lever.

Nevertheless there is a very acceptable degree of quality about the car and its fittings. The carpets are of good quality, the dashboard is fully equipped—although both instruments and switches are somewhat haphazardly located. The dip switch is particularly badly placed.

The speedometer and rev counter are immediately in front of the driver, and are visible through the X-spoked spring steering wheel, which, it was noted with relief, has a black rim. There are total and trip mileage recorders, a combined oil pressure and water temperature gauge, and a fuel gauge on the passenger's side. This latter is completely concealed by the fob of the ignition switch.

Luggage accommodation is divided between the shallow boot, in which resides the spare wheel, and the space behind the front seats. There are two map pockets, but no dash locker. For long holiday trips additional accommodation for luggage might be valued.

After experience with the M.G. A extending to almost 1,000 miles, it was difficult to avoid becoming attached to it. It has a cheerful attraction which draws one to it. It will potter about in city traffic without complaint, or it will eat up the miles on the open road with a pleasant purposefulness. It is only 13 ft. long, 4 ft. 11¼ in. wide and 4 ft. 2 in. high, so that parking and garaging it are easy. As a car for business purposes it offers the good design and robust finish of a hard-working piece of machinery which can be relied on to do a good job day after day. Its only snag in this direction is the difficulty with which one enters or leaves it.

For pleasure motoring it is very hard to beat, so long as two seats are enough. It flatters the good driver, lets him enjoy himself and enters into the pleasure of the journey.

As tested, with an efficient Smith's heater, a screen washer, and wire wheels, it costs £1,158 15s. 9d. In standard form it costs £1,087 7s., of which £363 7s. is purchase tax. ★

The wire wheel takes up more locker space than the disc, and soft bags are preferable in any event. There is more room inside the car for luggage

More power
to your safety

NEW ⬡M⬡ ⬡G⬡ ⬡A⬡ *1600* Mk II

Every sports car enthusiast will welcome the extra power of the Mark II MGA 1600; new 1622 cc engine; new compression ratio; Lockheed disc brakes on the front wheels, a new and greater performance for your greater safety.

With the world-famous M.G. 'Safety Fast' features of wonderful braking, stable cornering and fine road holding, this delightful performer is "As fine a car as it looks". That will be *your* verdict when you have a trial run.

12 Months' Warranty and backed by B.M.C. Service—the most comprehensive in Europe.

Price: £663 plus £305.2.3 P.T. *including surcharge.*

Safety Fast !

THE M.G. CAR COMPANY LIMITED, SALES DIVISION, COWLEY, OXFORD
London Showrooms : Stratton House, 80 Piccadilly, London, W.1. *Overseas Business :* Nuffield Exports Limited, Cowley, Oxford and 41 Piccadilly, London, W.1

37

THE M.G.A is an old friend to the readers of AUTOSPORT. I tested the original prototype EX182 long before it was in production, and the 1,500 c.c. version of the car was tried in open and coupé form. Now, this well-loved model has had a face lift, and the engine has been stretched to the 1,600 c.c. class, which is a popular category for competition purposes. Disc brakes have been standardized for the front wheels, and the sidescreens now incorporate sliding windows.

The M.G. is completely conventional. It has a rugged box-section frame, suspended in front on wishbones and helical springs, and the steering is by rack and pinion. The Lockheed hydraulic brakes

JOHN BOLSTER TESTS

The M.G.A 1600

A Lively Two-Seater of Pleasing Performance

are of disc type, 11 ins. diameter in front, and the rear 10 ins. drums are on a hypoid axle, suspended on semi-elliptic springs.

Based on the B.M.C. "A" series unit, the engine is a conventional four-cylinder with pushrod operated overhead valves. A small increase in the bore has put the capacity up from 1,489 c.c. to 1,588 c.c. A power bonus of some 6 b.h.p. has been secured, but more important is the raising of the torque curve in the middle range of revolutions. The twin SU carburetters are of the H4 size, and an 8 ins. Borg and Beck clutch is well able to handle the power output. The gearbox, with its traditional short remote control lever, gives a high third speed, which has for long been an M.G. feature.

The steel body has modern lines, and it is very solidly constructed. The driver and passenger sit right down inside it on their separate seats, divided by a very

deep propeller shaft tunnel. The hood is attractive in appearance and folds neatly away behind the seats, this operation being best performed by two people. There is a good array of instruments, and the bumpers give real protection, the overriders being quite massive.

On taking over the car, one is at once impressed by the long, low appearance, the attractive finish, and the many practical details. Accessibility for normal maintenance is generally satisfactory, though this does not apply to the battery. Unfortunately, I must once again award a black mark to the luggage boot, which has insufficient capacity for normal touring unless one leaves the spare wheel behind.

As one expects of an M.G., the driving position is good. The gear lever is ideally placed, and the all-round visibility belies the low driving position.

CONVENTIONAL four-cylinder push-rod engine powers the car, with twin car-buretters. LEFT: Driving position is good, the gear lever being ideally placed. Visibility is excellent.

The seats are comfortable for long journeys, though a little better lateral location would be appreciated. The instruments are well situated and legible, and the pedal arrangement makes the best use of the limited space available.

The engine is an instant starter and pulls well almost at once. The extra torque of the slightly bigger unit renders the car more flexible, and one makes less use of the gear lever than formerly during normal touring. Considered as a fast touring car, the M.G. must be rated very highly indeed. The occupants are well protected and the machine is comfortably sprung. It covers the ground in an effortless manner, and useful average speeds may be maintained without any feeling of strain.

At low speeds the steering feels rather dead and is perhaps heavier than would be expected. At higher velocities, however, it comes into its own, being

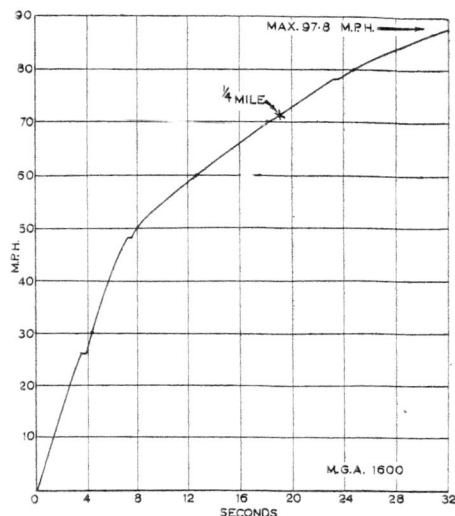

ACCELERATION GRAPH

delightfully accurate and affording a fine sense of control. The gearbox is a splendid component, and it would be hard to better the easy and precise operation of that short and rigid lever. The clutch is well able to cope with the bigger engine; the brakes also are entirely free from vice and cannot be made to fade.

The engine cruises at high speeds or revs happily on the indirect gears with equal aplomb. However, as the maximum speed of the car is approached it does go through a rough period when both noise and vibration become somewhat pronounced. The test car failed to reach a genuine 100 m.p.h., but with a smooth hard top that figure should be attained without difficulty. The hood is not ideally streamlined and tends to flap at high speeds, so the wind resistance must be fairly high.

The car is definitely livelier than its predecessor, and perhaps the acceleration figures scarcely do justice to the increase in performance. This is because there is a rather marked tendency for one rear wheel to spin at the getaway, even on dry concrete. It is, in fact, necessary to be well on the move before full throttle can be applied on first gear. When the speed begins to rise, however, the very real benefit of the powerful engine can be felt.

Although the M.G. is primarily a sports-touring car of the high speed variety, many amateur drivers will employ it for club racing. Accordingly, I drove the car to its limit on a racing circuit. Under these conditions it remains very controllable at all times, and it would take a clumsy driver indeed to run out of road. The cornering power is not outstandingly high by competition standards, the M.G. being somewhat heavily built for such capers. For the man who primarily wants a fast road car, and does the odd club event on the side, this machine will provide an acceptable compromise.

The very solidity of the car's construction is apparent to driver and passenger alike, and is somewhat reassuring under modern traffic conditions. The whole basis of the vehicle is its immensely rigid chassis, and this no doubt has a

LONG, LOW appearance of the car and its attractive finish are immediately impressive on taking over the machine.

COCKPIT is well laid out, all instruments being easily readable. Curiously, no ammeter is fitted in spite of the full instrumentation.

SPECIFICATION AND PERFORMANCE DATA

Car Tested: M.G.A 1600 sports 2-seater. Price £940 7s. 6d. (including P.T.). Radio and heater extra.

Engine: Four cylinders 75.39 mm. x 88.9 mm. (1,588 c.c.), pushrod operated overhead valves. Compression ratio 8.3 to 1. 78 b.h.p. at 5,500 r.p.m. Twin SU carburetters. Lucas coil and distributor.

Transmission: Borg and Beck 8 ins. clutch. Four-speed gearbox with synchromesh on upper three speeds and central remote control lever, ratios 4.3, 5.908, 9.52, and 15.652 to 1. Open Hardy Spicer propeller shaft. Hypoid rear axle.

Chassis: Box-section frame. Independent front suspension by wishbones and helical springs.

great deal to do with its accurate steering and controllability. The doors are wide, to give reasonably easy entry to the low car, and there are no outside door handles, it being necessary to slide the window forward and find the cord inside the door. The test car had pierced bolt-on disc wheels, but the knock-on type may be specified as an optional extra.

The M.G.A 1600 is a fast sports car

Rear axle on semi-elliptic springs. Piston-type hydraulic dampers. Lockheed hydraulic brakes with 11 ins. front discs and 10 ins. rear drums with fly-off hand brake. Bolt-on disc wheels fitted 5.60-15 ins. tyres.

Equipment: 12-volt lighting and starting. Speedometer. Rev. counter. Fuel, oil pressure, and water temperature gauges. Flashing indicators. Heater and radio (extra).

Dimensions: Wheelbase, 7 ft. 10 ins. Track, front 3 ft. 11½ ins., rear 4 ft. 0¾ in. Overall length 13 ft. Width 4 ft. 10 ins. Weight 18 cwt.

Performance: Maximum speed 97.8 m.p.h. Speeds in gears, 3rd 77 m.p.h., 2nd 50 m.p.h., 1st 26 m.p.h. Standing quarter-mile 19.2 secs. Acceleration: 0-30 m.p.h., 4.4 secs.; 0-50 m.p.h., 8 secs.; 0-60 m.p.h., 12.8 secs.; 0-80 m.p.h., 24.8 secs.

Fuel Consumption: 26 m.p.g.

that may almost be described as luxurious. It is lively, flexible, and a pleasure to drive, responding admirably to the proper use of that delightful gear lever but being perfectly willing to co-operate if one is in a lazy mood. It is, in fact, as practical a mode of everyday transport as many more staid vehicles, and its fade-free brakes, snappy acceleration and good road-holding are all important safety features.

The M.G. A Hardtop Coupé

An Economical 100 m.p.h. Car with Exceptional Roadworthiness

IN the world of motoring there are many cars capable of exceeding 100 m.p.h.; indeed, most current American productions are capable of this feat. In contrast, the majority of European cars place an accent on economical running as exemplified by a fuel consumption of, say, better than 25 m.p.g. Standing between these two extremes there is a choice of four cars, all of European origin, which will beat by a useful margin both the 100 m.p.h. and the 25 m.p.g. mark, the latest recruit to this select company being the M.G. A model with the fixed-head coupé body.

Reference to our road test of the car in original form with open body but raised hood will show that the maximum speed on a flat and level road was 97.8 m.p.h., but the coupé model recently tested on the banked Montlhéry track displayed a sensibly superior performance by returning an overall lap time equivalent to 101.2 m.p.h with a fastest half kilometre at 103.8 m.p.h. There is therefore no question of the

ability of this car to exceed the three figure mark and anyone who questions the utility of this feat in itself should consider the implications thereof upon acceleration in the upper speed ranges and in the ability to cruise with the engine running on a modest throttle opening.

So far as acceleration is concerned, the figures show that making full use of the gearbox the M.G. will run up to 80 m.p.h. within 25 sec. from a speed of 40 m.p.h. and even if the driver remains in top gear between these two speeds the time needed is only 30 sec. A speed of 80 m.p.h. is therefore readily within the compass of the car on any reasonable section of road and in this condition the piston speed is only slightly in excess of 2,500 ft/min. and the engine is delivering little more than half maximum power.

The high acceleration of the car is perhaps of particular value on British roads; the aspect of a comfortable 80 m.p.h. cruising is of especial value abroad and it is perhaps significant that an extremely high proportion of M.G. A. production is exported.

Road surfaces abroad are notoriously poorer than they are in England and for this reason we were particularly impressed by the robustness of the car and the entire absence of chassis wave or body shake even when speeds considerably greater than 80 m.p.h. were being sustained on Continental highways. This high stiffness factor not only ensures freedom from deterioration of door windows, window frames and other small items in the general structure but also gives the driver and passenger a psychological impression that high speeds can be maintained in safety, whereas some more flimsily built vehicles suffer not only from mechanical disabilities

but also impose strain and anxiety upon the occupants.

The impression of safety engendered by the M.G. is, fortunately, founded on fact. Although with the recommended tyre pressures, squeal is somewhat prevalent with high-speed cornering, with the higher pressures adopted on Montlhéry circuit, this annoyance disappears, and cornering power comes up into the racing car class which is not particularly surprising in view of the 30 years' continuous competition experience which lies behind the car.

Although automobile engineering has reached the point where the maximum speed acceleration and fuel consumption of a new car will conform closely to predictions derived from the drawing board, this is by no means true in regard to steering and handling characteristics and the prototype M.G. A. models were developed on a special course to a point where the speed through a given series of corners was equal to the best obtainable irrespective of selling price.

The coupé displays almost neutral steering characteristics coupled with exceptional rapidity of response under the influence of the absolutely positive rack and pinion steering gear. The steering wheel itself might perhaps be placed farther from the driver for the benefit of those who prefer the modern straight-arm control position and over rough surfaces there is noticeable shake on the wheel which does not in any way affect the straight running of the vehicle. By the standards of the family car more than usual physical effort has to be exerted on the wheel, but this is a very small price to pay for that feeling of absolute mastery over the attitude of the vehicle which is one of the most desirable features a car

In Brief
Price (including wire wheels, heater, screen washer, etc., as tested), plus purchase tax: £1,158 15s. 9d.
Basic price of £724, with 363 7s. 0d. purchase tax equals £1,087 7s. 0d.
Capacity ... ... 1,489 c.c.
Unladen kerb weight ... 18½ cwt.
Acceleration:
  20-40 m.p.h. in top gear ... 13.6 sec.
  0-50 m.p.h. through gears ... 10.8 sec.
Maximum direct top gear
  gradient ... ... 1 in 10.7
Maximum speed ... ...101.2 m.p.h.
"Maximile" speed ... 92 m.p.h.
Touring fuel consumption ... 31.5 m.p.g.
Gearing: 17 m.p.h. in top gear at 1,000 r.p.m.; 29 m.p.h. at 1,000 ft./min. piston speed.

SEATS which are rather low-set in relation to the scuttle are nevertheless very comfortable and give good lateral support; there is a central armrest on the transmission tunnel and, on the car tested, an optionally extra ashtray. Just forward of this is the stubby gearlever which gives very pleasant, positive use of the gearbox.

haps reduced by the wire wheels fitted.

It is clear from the very good figures recorded in the data panel and the remarks which have been so far made that the M.G. coupé is a car of considerable merit. It is also one which quickly commands affection by reason of those qualities of pleasure in driving and comfort in travelling which are not necessarily the outcome of good engineering. The suspension is on the hard side and this fact is the more noticeable if the tyres are run on the higher limits of pressure. If, however, bumps are somewhat more than usually noticeable neither pitch nor roll can normally be discerned and long high-speed journeys cause little physical and no mental fatigue.

Comfort could be further improved by raising the seats an inch or two which would at the same time give a better view over the rather high scuttle, as with the standard position a person of moderate height scarcely has both wings of the car in view. But the seats themselves are comfortable and give good support against side forces, a large fore and aft travel making it possible to accommodate small packages or even suitcases in the well at the back of the cockpit. The inboard mounting of the spare wheel causes an intrusion which is particularly noticeable in the somewhat shallow rear locker and for serious touring it would certainly be necessary to fit the optionally offered external luggage rack. Other minor matters which justify criticism are the somewhat limited arcs swept by the windscreen wipers and a rather haphazard layout of instruments and switches, although the principal items of road and

can have and yet is so rarely experienced.

The clutch gives a firm take up and very rapid gear changes can be made, despite the rather wide gap between top and third gear, the speed on the latter being restricted to 70 m.p.h. unless the driver is prepared to take the tachometer needle past the 5,500 r.p.m. mark into the red section. When the acceleration figures were obtained the needle was kept below this area and if the maximum r.p.m. had been increased to the competition limit of 6,000 r.p.m. slightly better times might have been recorded.

As a counterpart to the somewhat wide gap between top and third gear the latter is an excellent ratio to use either in traffic or on country roads as it gives very vivid acceleration between 10 and 60 m.p.h., some pinking from the engine however being noticeable below 2,000 r.p.m. unless 100 octane fuel is used.

The engine cannot be called mechanically quiet. There is a rattle from the pushrod valvegear which is an established characteristic of the type and does not denote mechanical defect but the gearbox and rear axle are free from objectionable noise. The attraction of the fully open car cannot be denied and the name M.G. is especially identified with this type. Nevertheless, from a strictly practical point of view it must be pointed out that despite the introduction of wind-down windows and wraparound rear window the coupé M.G. went on the scales only 32 lb. heavier than the open type; it is 3½ m.p.h. faster and returns a fuel consumption 1 m.p.g. better. Any resonant effects which may be introduced by the use of a closed body are more than offset by the reduced wind noise and buffeting which follow from the enclosure of the occupants and by reason of a well-designed and carefully positioned wraparound windscreen.

The overall fuel consumption was based upon hard driving (including some 50 laps

of the Montlhéry circuit) but the M.G., by reason of the characteristics set out above encourages the driver to make full use of the performance available, this procedure being also wholly acceptable to the passenger.

Should it be necessary to drive really hard the brakes will be found equal to all demands made upon them, pedal pressures being reasonable, stopping consistent and free from the generation of smoke or smell, the drum temperatures being per-

TWO inclined S.U. carburetters feed mixture to the four-cylinder o.h.v. engine. Plugs, coil, advance and retard unit, dipstick, carburetters and oil filler are easy to reach.

EXCELLENT rearward visibility follows from the use of a wrapround rear window which in conjunction with big door windows reduces the "blind" quarters to a near-minimum.

WITH spare wheel and tool roll carried in the boot, little room is left for luggage, but there is additional space behind the seats and an external luggage rack is available as an extra.

ted the entrance of rain water as well as raising the noise level.

No car is perfect and these minor criticisms must be viewed against the background that this is a car in which the exceptional performance, safety and pleasure are derived from simple mechanical components in large-scale production. In consequence, spares and maintenance costs are not out of line with ordinary commercial practice and no special mechanical skill or tuning aptitude is needed to keep the car in 100% mechanical condition. The accessibility of the engine components is adequate and an inspection of the chassis shows that the running gear is exceptionally robust and that the number of points needing regular lubrication has been reduced to nine.

Moderately priced, economical to run and maintain, remarkably fast, exceptionally safe and above all a constant pleasure to drive and be driven in, it is not surprising that the M.G. A is beating all production records at Abingdon and that it has established itself as the most popular sports car in the world.

engine speed are clearly displayed immediately before the driver.

A nearside door lock is logical enough for the bulk of cars sold with left-hand drive but for the home market a lock on the driver's door would be more appropriate and as in a closed car, the driver would probably not wear headgear, the

absence of a sun vizor is hard to excuse.

The car tested had a built-in heater and ventilator which seemed more successful at supplying heated air, which was unwanted at this time of year, than fresh air at ambient temperature; which was more to be regretted as opening either the side windows or the ventilating panels permit-

Specification

Engine

Cylinders	...	...	...	4
Bore	...	...	...	73.025 mm.
Stroke	...	...	...	89 mm.
Cubic capacity	...	...	...	1,489 c.c.
Piston area	...	...	...	25.97 sq. in.
Valves	...	...	Pushrod o.h.v.
Compression ratio	...	...	8.3/1
Carburetters	...	Two inclined S.U. 1½ in.
Fuel pump	...	S.U. electrical, rear-mounted
Ignition timing control	...	...	Vacuum
Oil filter	...	...	Full flow Tecalemit
Max. power (net)	...	...	72 b.h.p.
at	...	...	5,500 r.p.m.
Piston speed at max. b.h.p.	3,220 ft./min.

Transmission

Clutch	...	...	...	Single dry plate
Top gear (s/m)	...	...	...	4.3
3rd gear (s/m)	...	...	...	5.908
2nd gear (s/m)	...	...	...	9.52
1st gear	...	...	...	15.652
Reverse	...	...	...	20.468
Propeller shaft	...	...	Open
Final drive	...	...	Hypoid bevel
Top gear m.p.h. at 1,000 r.p.m.	17
Top gear m.p.h. at 1,000 ft./min. piston speed	...	...	29

Chassis

Brakes	...Lockheed hydraulic (2 l.s. front)
Brake drum internal diameter	...	10 in.
Friction lining area	...	...	134.4 sq. in.
Suspension:				
Front	...	Coil and wishbone, i.f.s.
Rear	...	...	Semi-elliptic
Shock absorbers:				
Front	...	Armstrong incorporated in upper wishbone pivots
Rear	...	...	Armstrong hydraulic
Steering gear	...	...	Rack and pinion
Tyres	...	...	Dunlop 5.60—15

Coachwork and Equipment

Starting handle	...	...	...	Yes
Battery mounting	...	...	Behind seats
Jack	...	...	...	Screw-type
Jacking points	...	...	Front wishbones and rear springs

Standard tool kit: Ring-type tappet spanner, wheelbrace (copper hammer with wire wheels), tappet gauge, sparking plug spanner, pliers, grease gun, adjustable spanner, 2 tyre levers, cylinder head nut spanner, tyre valve spanner, distributor screwdriver and gauge, tyre pump, 3 box spanners, 3 o/e spanners, screwdriver, recessed screwdriver, tommy bar, jack, brake bleeder tube, gearbox plug spanner, touch-up paint-pencil, tool roll.

Exterior lights: 2 head, 2 side-indicator, 2 rear/brake/indicator.

Number of electrical fuses	...	...	Two
Direction indicators	...	Flashing type, self-cancelling
Windscreen wipers	...	Electric, self-parking
Windscreen washers	...	...	Optional
Sun vizors	...	...	...	No

Instruments: Speedometer with decimal trip distance recorder, rev. counter, oil pressure gauge, water thermometer.

Warning lights	...	Ignition, indicators, headlamp main beam
Locks:			
With ignition key	...	...	Ignition
With other keys	...	...	None
Glove lockers	...	...	None
Map pockets	...	...	Two
Parcel shelves	...	...	None
Ashtrays	...	One between seats
Cigar lighters	...	...	None
Interior lights	...	Instrument panel, map-reading light

Interior heater   Fresh-air type with de-mister

Car radio	...	Optional, Radiomobile

Extras available: Radio, heater, wire wheels, fog lamp, white-wall tyres, 4.55/1 axle gears, twin horns, external luggage carrier, radiator blind, rim embellishers, telescopic steering column, screen-washer, badge bar.

Upholstery material	Leather over foam rubber
Floor covering	...	Carpet
Exterior colours standardized	5
Alternative body styles	...	Open 2-seater

Maintenance

Sump	...	...	...	6½ pints, S.A.E. 30
Gearbox	...	...	4 pints, S.A.E. 30
Rear axle	...	...	2¾ pints, Hypoid 90
Steering gear lubricant	...	Hypoid 90
Cooling system capacity	10 pints (2 drain taps)
Chassis lubrication	...	By grease gun every 1,000 miles to 9 points
Ignition timing	...	...	7° b.t.d.c.
Contact-breaker gap	...	.014-.016 in.
Sparking plug gap	...	...	.019-.021 in.

Valve timing: I.o. 16° b.t.d.c.; i.c. 56° a.b.d.c.; e.o. 51° b.b.d.c.; e.c. 21° a.t.d.c.

Tappet clearances (hot)	...	...	.017 in.
Front wheel toe-in	...	..	...	Nil
Camber angle	...	...	...	1°
Castor angle	...	...	...	4°
Tyre pressures:				
Front	...	...	...	17 lb.
Rear	...	...	...	20 lb.
(Fast driving, 18 lb. and 23 lb.)				
Brake fluid	...	...	...	Lockheed

Battery type and capacity... Lucas SG9E, 12-v.

Miscellaneous: Tyre pressures as inflated for high speeds 22 lb. and 26 lb.

The **Motor** Road Test No. 30/57 (Continental)

Make: M.G. **Type:** M.G. A Coupé

Makers: M.G. Car Co. Ltd., Abingdon-on-Thames, Berkshire

Test Data

CONDITIONS: *Weather : Wind 10 to 15 m.p.h; showery. (Temperature 78°F., Barometer 29.6 in. Hg.). Surface : Concrete : Montlhery Track. Fuel : British and French Premium.*

INSTRUMENTS

Speedometer at 30 m.p.h.	3% fast
Speedometer at 60 m.p.h.	3% fast
Speedometer at 90 m.p.h.	4% fast
Speedometer at 100 m.p.h.	7% fast
Distance recorder	accurate

WEIGHT :

Kerb weight (unladen, but with oil, coolant and fuel for approx. 50 miles) .. .. 18½ cwt.
Front/rear distribution of kerb weight 52/48
Weight laden as tested .. .. 21¾ cwt.

MAXIMUM SPEEDS

Flying Montlhéry Lap .. .. 101.2 m.p.h.
Best one-way ¼-km. time equals .. 103.8 m.p.h.
"Maximile" Speed. (Timed quarter-mile after one mile accelerating from rest.)
Mean of four runs .. .. 92.0 m.p.h.
Best one-way time equals .. .. 94.8 m.p.h.
Speed in Gears at recommended limit of 5,500 r.p.m.
Max. speed in third .. .. .. 68 m.p.h.
Max. speed in second .. .. .. 42 m.p.h.
Max. speed in first .. .. .. 26 m.p.h.

FUEL CONSUMPTION

47.0 m.p.g. at constant 40 m.p.h. on level.
43.2 m.p.g. at constant 50 m.p.h. on level.
35.4 m.p.g. at constant 60 m.p.h. on level.
31.2 m.p.g. at constant 70 m.p.h. on level.
28.8 m.p.g. at constant 80 m.p.h. on level.
24.8 m.p.g. at constant 90 m.p.h. on level.
Overall Fuel Consumption for 742 miles, 26.9 gallons, equals 27.6 m.p.g. (10.2 litres/100 km.).
Touring Fuel Consumption (m.p.g. at steady speed midway between 30 m.p.h. and maximum, less 5% allowance for acceleration) 31.5 m.p.g.
Fuel Tank Capacity (makers' figure) 10 gallons.

STEERING

Turning circle between kerbs :
Left .. .. 28½ feet
Right .. .. 29¼ feet
Turns of steering wheel from lock to lock 2¾

BRAKES from 30 m.p.h.

0.94g retardation (equivalent to 32 ft. stopping distance) with 90 lb. pedal pressure.
0.80g retardation (equivalent to 37½ ft. stopping distance) with 75 lb. pedal pressure.
0.52g retardation (equivalent to 58 ft. stopping distance) with 50 lb. pedal pressure.
0.27g retardation (equivalent to 115 ft. stopping distance) with 25 lb. pedal pressure.

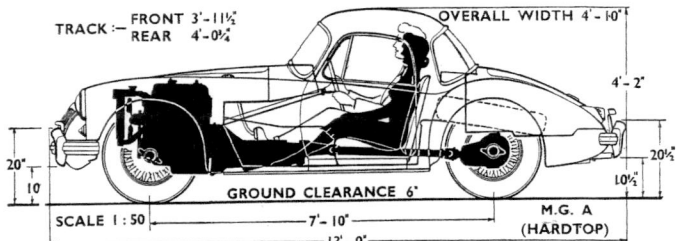

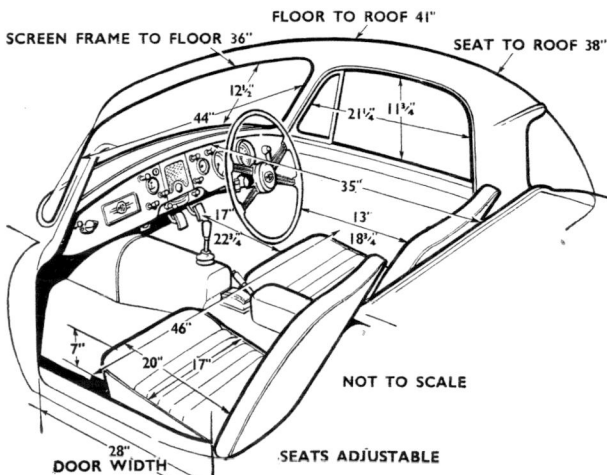

TRACK :— FRONT 3'-11½" REAR 4'-0¾"
OVERALL WIDTH 4'-10"
4'-2"
20½"
10½"
20"
10
GROUND CLEARANCE 6"
SCALE 1 : 50 — 7'-10" —
— 13'-0" —
M.G. A (HARDTOP)

FLOOR TO ROOF 41"
SCREEN FRAME TO FLOOR 36"
SEAT TO ROOF 38"
12½"
44"
21¼" 11¾"
35"
17"
13"
18¾"
22¼"
46"
7"
20" 17"
28" DOOR WIDTH
SEATS ADJUSTABLE
NOT TO SCALE

ACCELERATION TIMES from standstill

0-30 m.p.h.	5.0 sec.
0-40 m.p.h.	7.2 sec.
0-50 m.p.h.	10.8 sec.
0-60 m.p.h.	15.7 sec.
0-70 m.p.h.	21.4 sec.
0-80 m.p.h.	32.1 sec.
Standing quarter mile	19.8 sec.

ACCELERATION TIMES on upper ratios

	Top gear	3rd gear
10-30 m.p.h.	13.6 sec.	8.1 sec.
20-40 m.p.h.	13.6 sec.	7.9 sec.
30-50 m.p.h.	13.8 sec.	8.1 sec.
40-60 m.p.h.	12.6 sec.	8.7 sec.
50-70 m.p.h.	13.7 sec.	10.4 sec.
60-80 m.p.h.	17.6 sec.	—
70-90 m.p.h.	28.1 sec.	—

HILL CLIMBING at sustained steady speeds.

Max. gradient on top .. .. 1 in 10.7 (Tapley 210 lb./ton)
Max. gradient on third .. 1 in 7.3 (Tapley 305 lb./ton)
Max. gradient on second .. 1 in 4.75 (Tapley 472 lb./ton)

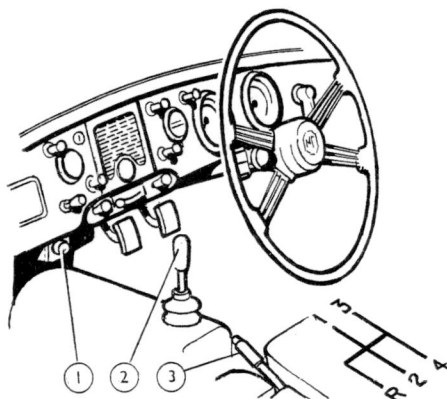

1, Headlamp dip switch. 2, Gear lever. 3, Handbrake. 4, Bonnet catch release. 5, Fuel contents gauge. 6, Windscreen washer control. 7, Choke control. 8, Ventilator control. 9, Temperature and heater fan switch. 10, Horn button. 11, Demisting control. 12, Starter button. 13, Water thermometer. 14, Dynamo charge warning light. 15, Trip re-setting knob. 16, Headlamp main beam indicator light. 17, Map reading light switch. 18, Map reading light. 19, Windscreen wipers switch. 20, Ignition switch. 21, Oil pressure gauge. 22, Lights switch. 23, Fog lamp switch. 24, Tachometer. 25, Panel light switch. 26, Speedometer and distance recorder. 27, Direction indicator switch. 28, Direction indicator warning light.

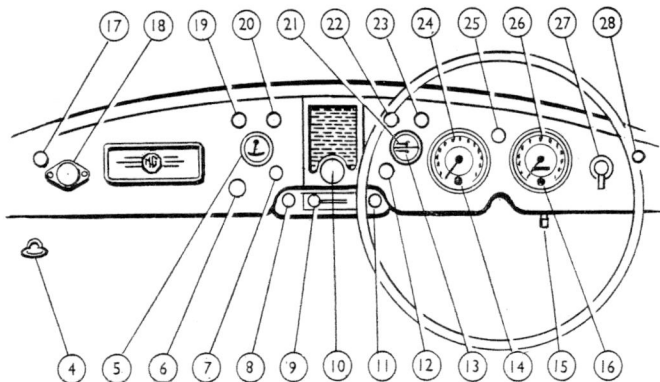

M.G.
M.G.A. 1600 — 1959-1960

The M.G.A. 1600 is basically the same as the superseded M.G.A. and the following details are those modifications effected in the change of models. For further complete details see the preceding M.G.A. 1956-1959 Section.

NOTE: All dimensions are in inches unless otherwise specified

ENGINE

GENERAL.

Engine type: B.M.C., 16GA, 4-cylinder, in line, O.H.V. Nominal bore: 2.968. Stroke: 3.5. Cubic capacity: 96.9 cu. ins. (1,588 c.c.). Compression ratio: 8.3 to 1.

SPARKING PLUGS.

Make and type: Champion N5 — 14 mm. Electrode gap: 0.24 to .026. Firing order: 1, 3, 4, 2.

DISTRIBUTOR.

Make and type: Lucas — DM2; later models DM2 P4. Contact point gap: .014 to .016. Ignition timing: 6° B.T.D.C.

CARBURETTER.

Make and type: S.U. twin H4 semi-downdraught. Diameter: 1½ inches. Needle: No. 6. Jet: .090. Piston damper spring: Red.

PISTON RINGS.

Compression: Plain top ring; tapered 2nd and 3rd. Width: .0615 to .0625. Thickness: .141 to .148. Fitted gap: .009 to .014. Clearance in groove: .0015 to .0035.

Oil control: Slotted scraper. Width: .1552 to .1562. Thickness: .135 to .142. Gap fitted: .009 to .014. Clearance in groove: .0016 to .0036.

CONNECTING RODS.

Length between centres: 6.50. Big end bearing side clearance: .008 to .012. Big end bearing running clearance: .001 to .0025.

VALVES AND VALVE GEAR.

Valve lift: .350. Valve stem to guide clearance: Inlet .00155 to .00255; exhaust .002 to .003.

Rocker arm to valve clearance: .015 (hot). Clearance for valve timing: .060.

Valve guide length: Inlet 1⅞; exhaust 2¹³⁄₆₄. Valve guide diameter: Outside .5635 to .5640; inside .34425 to .34475.

Valve guide fitted height above head: .625.

LUBRICATION.

Oil pressure (normal running): Minimum 15 p.s.i.; maximum 50 p.s.i.

FRONT SUSPENSION

Coil spring details:—

Coil diameter (mean): 3.28. Wire diameter: .54. Free length: 8.88 ±1/16. Number of free coils: 7.2. Static laden length: 6.60 ±1/32. Load at laden length: 1,095 lbs. ±20 lbs. Maximum deflection: 4 inches.

P—(Int)

BRAKES

Make and type: Lockheed hydraulic; front, disc; rear, drum.

Lining material: DON.24. Disc material: Capex 4. Lining length: 9.63. Lining width: 1.7. Total lining area (rear): 65.48 sq. ins. Disc diameter (front): 11 inches.

33—L.H. tail lamp.
34—Number plate lamp.
35—R.H. tail lamp.
36—Stop lamp switch.
37—L.H. stop lamp.
38—R.H. stop lamp.
39—Heater switch (when fitted)
40—Heater motor.
41—Fuel gauge.
42—Fuel tank unit.
43—Flasher unit.
44—L.H. rear flasher.
45—L.H. front flasher.
46—Flasher switch.
47—R.H. front flasher.
48—R.H. rear flasher.
49—Flasher warning light.
50—Windshield wiper switch.
51—Windshield wiper motor.
52—Fuel pump.
53—Ignition coil.
54—Distributor.
55—Snap connectors.
56—Terminal blocks or junction box.
57—Earth connections made via cable.
58—Earth connections made via fixing bolts.

Cable Colour Code:

R—Red.   B—Black.
S—Slate.   U—Blue.
W—White.   N—Brown.
Y—Yellow. G—Green.
D—Dark.   K—Pink.
L—Light.   P—Purple.
M—Medium.

When a cable has two colour code letters the first denotes the main colour and the second denotes the tracer colour.

1—Generator.
2—Control box.
3—Two 6-volt batteries.
4—Ignition warning light.
5—Ignition switch.
6—Starter switch.
7—Starter motor.
8—R.H. fog lamp (if fitted).
9—L.H. fog lamp.
10—Main beam warning light.
11—R.H. headlamp main beam.
12—L.H. headlamp main beam.
13—L.H. headlamp dip beam.
14—R.H. headlamp dip beam.
15—L.H. pilot lamp.
16—R.H. pilot lamp.
17—Lighting switch.
18—Fog lamp switch.
19—Dipper switch.
20—Horn.
21—Fuse unit.
22—Twin wind-tone horns (if fitted).
23—Horn push.
24—Panel lamp rheostat.
25—Panel lamp.
26—Panel lamp.
27—Panel lamp.
28—Panel lamp.
29—Map lamp switch.
30—Map lamp.
31—Headlamp flick relay.
32—Headlamp flick switch.

Wiring diagram.

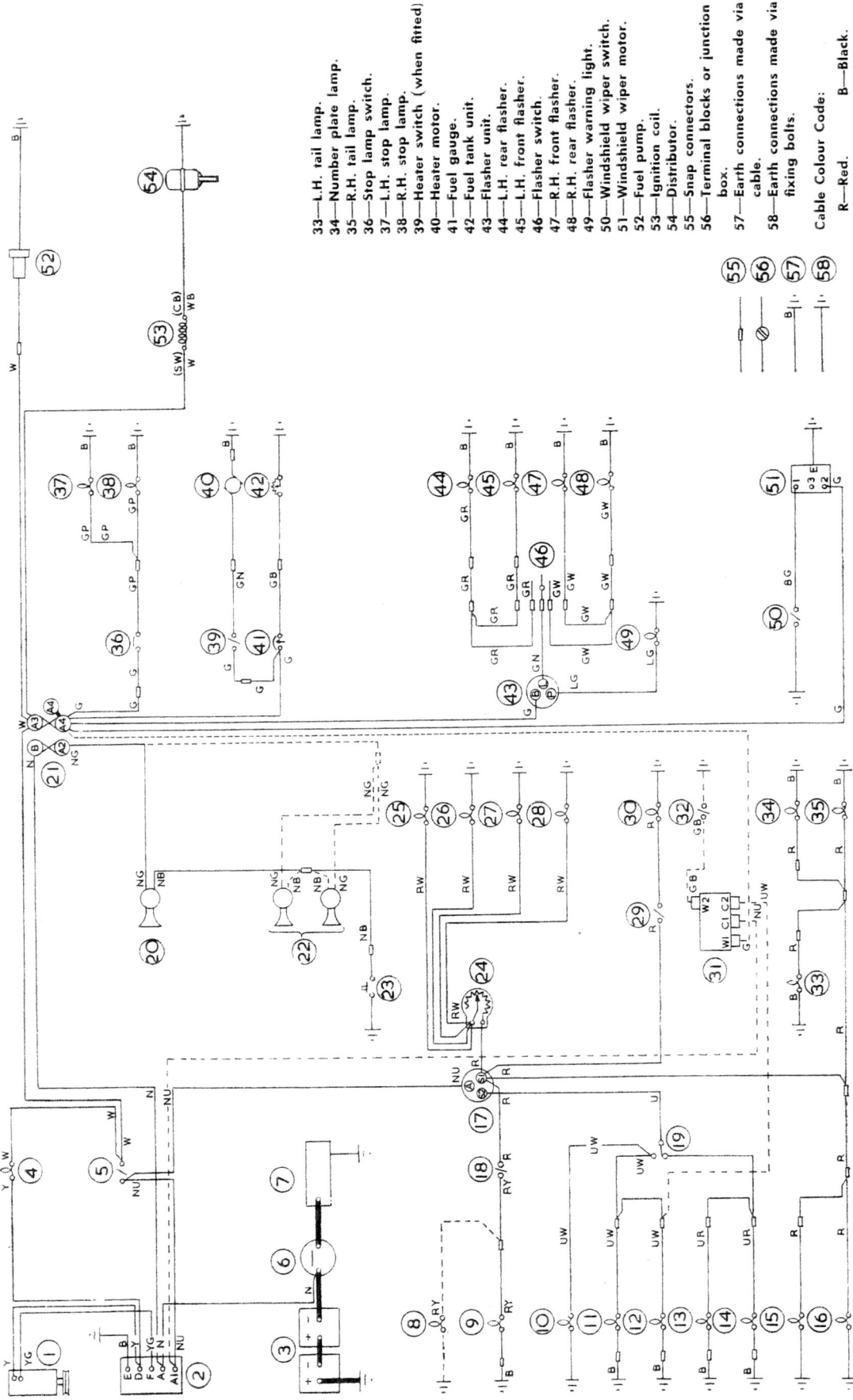

45

M.G.
M.G.A. TWIN CAM — 1958-1960

NOTE: All dimensions are in inches unless otherwise specified

TUNE UP

GENERAL.

Engine type: 4-cylinder, twin O.H.C. Nominal bore: 2.969. Stroke: 3.5. Cubic capacity: 96.906 cu. ins. (1,588 c.c.). Compression ratio: 9.9 to 1.

SPARKING PLUGS.

Make and type: Champion N3. Size: 14 mm. Point gap: .025. Firing order: 1, 3, 4, 2.

DISTRIBUTOR.

Make and type: Lucas DM2. Control: Centrifugal and vacuum advance. Breaker point gap: .014 to .016. Breaker arm spring tension: 20 to 24 ozs. Condenser capacity: .2 mfd. Initial timing: T.D.C.

VALVES.

Tappet to stem clearance (cold): Inlet and exhaust .016 to .017.

CARBURETTER.

Make and type: S.U. twin H6 semi-downdraught. Diameter: $1\frac{3}{4}$ inches. Needle: OA6. Jet: .10. Piston spring: Red, $4\frac{1}{2}$ ozs.

CAPACITIES (Imperial).

Engine and filter: 13 pints (15.6 U.S.). Gearbox: $4\frac{3}{4}$ pints (5.7 U.S.). Rear axle: $2\frac{3}{4}$ pints ($3\frac{1}{4}$ U.S.). Steering rack: $\frac{1}{2}$ pint (.6 U.S.). Cooling system: $13\frac{1}{2}$ pints (16.2 U.S.). Fuel tank: 10 gallons (12 U.S.).

TYRES.

Size: 5.90 x 15 inch. Normal pressure: Front 18 p.s.i.; rear 20 p.s.i. High speed driving: Front 22 p.s.i.; rear 24 p.s.i. Competition work: Front 24 p.s.i.; rear 26 p.s.i.

OIL FILTER.

Type: External full-flow.

BATTERY.

Check condition.

ELECTRICAL.

Check all lights, starter and dynamo operation, and other electrical items.

FUEL PUMP.

Make and type: S.U. LCS electric. Delivery test: 12.5 imp. gallons per hour. Suction lift: 33 inches. Output lift: 48 inches.

TORQUE FIGURES
IN POUNDS FEET,

Cylinder head studs: 70. Big end bearings bolts: 35. Main bearings studs: 70. Flywheel securing bolts: 35. Clutch pressure plate screws: 35 to 40. Crownwheel securing: 55 to 60. Differential bearing cap nuts: 60 to 65. Pinion flange nut: 135 to 140.

TOP OVERHAUL

VALVES.

Valve face angle: 45° inlet and exhaust. Valve seat angle: 45° inlet and exhaust. Valve head diameter: Inlet 1.59; exhaust 1.44. Stem diameter: .342 inlet and exhaust. Stem to guide clearance: .00155 to .00255 inlet and exhaust. Clearance at tappet (cold): .016 to .017 inlet and exhaust.

CYLINDER HEAD.

Two overhead camshafts are mounted on the cylinder head and some special procedure is necessary for removal and replacement. (See "Top Overhaul Notes".)

Two of the inlet manifold studs pass through the manifold and these nuts are inside the intakes as shown in Fig. 1.

Fig. 1.—Two of the manifold securing nuts (arrowed) are fitted inside the intakes.

The valve guides are of unequal length and shouldered and are removed by drifting through from the combustion chamber side.

CHECK ITEMS.

Check plugs, distributor, carburetter, fuel pump, as in "Tune Up".

NOTES.
CAMSHAFT DRIVING SPROCKETS.

When the camshafts or cylinder head are removed it is necessary to first disconnect the camshaft driving sprockets from the driving flanges on the camshafts. Proceed as follows:—

Remove the three setscrews, spring washers and plain washers securing the front end of each camshaft cover and the three domed nuts and copper washers along the top of the covers. Lift off the camshaft covers. Mark the camshaft sprockets and the driving flanges so that the sprockets may be replaced in their original positions on assembly.

Slacken the timing chain tensioner adjusting screw right off.

Remove the locking wire from the two setscrews securing each camshaft driving sprocket to the camshaft flange and slacken the screws. Slacken the two nuts securing the camshaft sprocket support plate to the timing chain cover. Pull the camshaft sprocket and support spindle away from the camshaft flange and engage the thread on the spindle away from the camshaft flange and engage the thread on the spindle with the support plate (see Fig. 2). Remove the driving sprocket setscrews completely.

When re-assembling the driving sprockets to the camshaft, line up the marks (made on removal) on the flanges before fitting the sprocket securing screws. Re-wire the screws after final tightening.

Fig. 3.—The correct order of tightening and slackening the cylinder head nuts.

TAPPET CLEARANCE.

If the engine is to give its best performance and the valves are to retain their maximum life it is essential to maintain the correct tappet clearances. Accordingly it is recommended that the clearance be checked at regular intervals and any necessary adjustments made.

The clearance for both inlet and exhaust valves is .016 to .017 when the engine is cold. The engine is designed to operate with this clearance and no departure from it is permissible.

The valve clearances are adjusted by means of hardened-steel shims interposed between the underside of each tappet and the top of the valve stem.

Turn the engine and check the clearance of each tappet with a feeler gauge. Care must be taken to ensure that the clearance is measured on the back of the cam, i.e., opposite the peak. Take note of the clearance figures.

Fig. 2.—The sprocket support spindle thread engaged in the support plate.

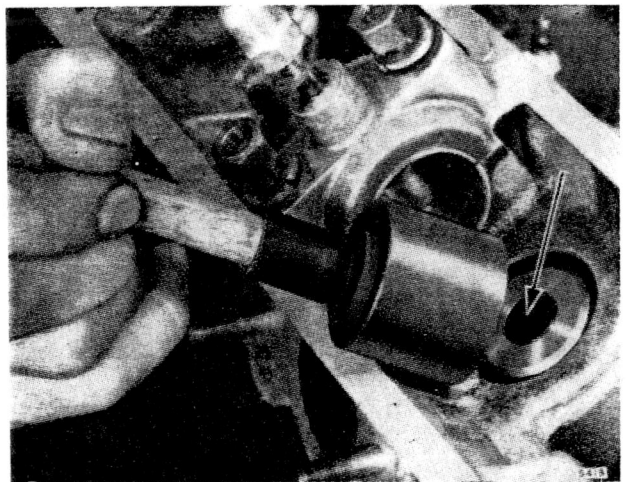

Fig. 4.—Withdrawing a tappet with a valve grinding suction tool. The adjusting shim is indicated by the arrow.

To adjust the tappet clearances disconnect the cam-shaft driving sprockets and remove the camshafts. Withdraw one of the tappets which requires adjustment, using a valve grinding suction tool (see Fig. 4), and remove the shim. Insert a new shim of suitable thickness to correct the valve clearance and replace the tappet. Correct the other valve clearances in a similar manner and replace the camshafts.

Recheck the valve clearances after finally tightening the camshaft bearing nuts, and carry out any further adjustments if necessary.

Variations in the tappet clearances have a marked influence upon the valve timing and it is, therefore, advisable to check the timing after adjusting the tappets.

The shims are available in 16 sizes and the thickness of a shim is indicated by a stamped number.

The numbers 1 to 16 correspond to sizes of .086 to .116 in increments of .002.

Fig. 5.—The camshaft locking tool in use. See Fig. 8 for dimensions.

ENGINE

CYLINDER BORES AND CRANKSHAFT.

Standard bore diameter: 2.9683 to 2.9698. Over-sizes for reboring: +.010, +.020, +.030, +.040. Main bearing journal diameter: 2.00. Minimum diameter for regrinding: 1.960. Main bearing journal length: 1.50. Crankshaft end float: .006 (max.) taken at centre main bearing. Big end bearing journal diameter: 1.8759 to 1.8764. Minimum diameter for regrinding: 1.8359. Main bearing running clearance: .002 to .0037. Big end bearing running clearance: .002 to .0037.

PISTONS AND CONNECTING RODS.

Piston skirt clearance: Top .0058 to .0083; bottom .0035 to .0066. Number of compression rings: 1 plain (top), 2 tapered (second and third). Number of oil control rings: 1 Microland scraper. Piston ring width: Compression .054 to .055; oil control .1552 to .1562. Piston ring thickness: Compression .124 to .131; oil control .124 to .131. Clearance in ring groove: Compression .0015 to .0035; oil control .0015 to .0035. Ring gap (fitted): .008 to .013.

Oversize pistons and rings available for reboring: +.010, +.020, +.030 and +.040.

Connecting rod length between centres: 6.5. Big end journal diameter (standard): 1.8759 to 1.8764. Minimum diameter for regrinding: 1.8359. Big end float: .008 to .012. Big end bearing running clearance: .002 to .0037. Gudgeon pin fit in connecting rod: Hand push fit at room temperature. Gudgeon pin fit in piston: Hand push fit at room temperature. Gudgeon pin diameter .875.

VALVES, GUIDES AND SPRINGS.

Valve guide bore diameter .3438 to .3443. Valve guide outside diameter .5645 to .5655. Valve guide length: Inlet $2\frac{1}{16}$; exhaust $2\frac{7}{16}$. Fitted height above cylinder head Inlet .750; exhaust .844. Valve head diameter Inlet 1.59; exhaust 1.44. Valve stem diameter Inlet .342; exhaust .342. Stem to guide clearance: .00155 to .00255. Seat angle on valve: Inlet 45°; exhaust 45°. Seat angle in cylinder head: Inlet 45°, exhaust 45°.

Valve timing: Inlet opens 20° B.T.D.C.; inlet closes 50° A.B.D.C.; exhaust opens 50° B.B.D.C.; exhaust closes 20° A.T.D.C. Running clearance at tappet (cold): .016 to .017.

Valve lift: .375. Valve spring free length: Inner 2.30; outer 2.54. Length fitted: Inner 1.62; outer 1.78. Spring pressure: Valve open, inner 65 lbs., outer 125 lbs.; valve closed, inner 42 lbs., outer 84 lbs.

CAMSHAFTS AND TAPPETS.

Camshaft journal diameter: 1.250 to 1.2505. Bearing number and type: 3. D2 bi-metal. Bearing inside diameter: 1.2515 to 1.2525. Running clearance: .001 to .0025. Camshaft end float: .001 to .005. Tappet diameter: 1.50. Tappet length: 1.25.

Fig. 6.—When replacing the timing gears the "T" markings must be in line as shown.

HALF-SPEED SHAFT.

Journal diameters: Front 1.78875 to 1.78925; centre 1.72875 to 1.72925; rear 1.62275 to 1.62325. End float: .003 to .006.

Bearing number and type: 3, Thinwall steel-backed white metal. Bearing inside diameter: Front 1.790; centre 1.730; rear 1.624. Running clearance: .001 to .002.

LUBRICATION.

Type of oil pump: Eccentric rotor. Relief valve operates: 50 p.s.i. Relief valve spring length: Free 3 inches; fitted $2\frac{5}{16}$ inches. Oil pressure: Normal 50 to 60 p.s.i.; idling 10 to 15 p.s.i.

CYLINDER HEAD.

See "Top Overhaul".

WATER PUMP.

The water pump is a centrifugal impeller type with two ball bearings separate from the shaft and a spring-loaded rubber seal assembly. The impeller and shaft assembly are removed from the rear of the pump and the bearings and distance tube from the front. Clearance between the front face of the impeller blades and the corresponding rear face of the pump body is .010 to .015.

OVERHAUL NOTES.

ENGINE REMOVAL.

Engine removal is straightforward leaving the gear-box in position, but it is necessary to remove the following components in addition to the more obvious ones: radiator, starter, steering column and dipper switch bracket.

Sling the engine so that it can be lifted slightly and moved forward and finally lifted up from the frame with the front considerably higher than the rear. Support the gearbox.

VALVE TIMING — CHECKING AND ADJUSTING.

Excessive stretch in the timing chain or variations in the tappet clearances will have a considerable effect on the valve timing and cause the performance of the car to suffer. The valve timing should, there-fore, be checked at regular intervals and adjusted if necessary.

Proceed as follows:—

Remove the camshaft covers and check the tappet clearances; adjust them if necessary.

Mount a dial indicator to a suitable fixed point on the cylinder head with the indicator foot rest-ing on No. 1 inlet valve tappet. Make certain that the cam is clear of the tappet and set the dial indi-cator to "O". Turn the engine until No. 1 piston is at T.D.C. with the valves rocking (i.e., No. 4

piston at T.D.C. on compression stroke) and line up the notch in the crankshaft pulley with the pro-jection in the timing cover.

If the timing of the inlet camshaft is correct the dial indicator will show that the tappet has moved between .069 to .082.

Set the dial indicator on No. 1 exhaust tappet and check in the same way. The exhaust tappet dis-placement should also be between .069 to .082.

If the timing is incorrect it can be reset in the following manner:—

Remove the timing chain cover. Knock back the tab-washer on the chain adjuster securing bolts and remove the chain adjuster. Swing the adjuster sprocket fork clear of the timing chain.

Turn the camshafts until the slots in the inner flanges line up with the slots in the front camshaft bearing housings. Lock both camshafts, using the tool described in Fig. 5.

Check that the "T" markings on the crankshaft and half-speed shaft gears are in their correct rela-tionship (see Fig. 6) and that No. 1 piston is at T.D.C.

Remove the camshaft sprocket securing screws and slacken the sprocket support spindles.

Turn the inlet camshaft sprocket in a clockwise direction to pull the timing chain tight between the half-speed shaft sprocket and the inlet camshaft sprocket. If two opposite holes in the sprocket do not line up exactly with the tapped holes in the camshaft flange, it will be necessary to use the vernier arrangement provided by the holes in the camshaft sprocket. The differential between one hole spacing and two wheel teeth is 1.2° of camshaft rotation.

Lift the chain away from the sprocket and turn the sprocket to select a pair of holes which will line up exactly with the tapped holes in the camshaft flange when the chain is tight.

When the correct holes have been selected, fit the sprocket securing screws and tighten the support spindle.

Remove the locking tool from the inlet camshaft.

Adjust the timing of the exhaust camshaft in a similar manner to that adopted for the inlet cam-shaft, ensuring that the **chain tension between the exhaust, inlet and half-speed shaft sprockets is retained.**

Fit the exhaust sprocket screws and tighten the support spindle.

Swing the sprocket adjuster fork to its correct position and replace the chain tensioner.

During the manufacture of the engine the sprocket and sprocket screws are marked "I" (inlet) and "X" (exhaust) to identify the holes which give the correct timing on assembly. These holes will not necessarily give the correct setting when the chain has stretched and should only be used for reference purposes.

Due to the vernier arrangement, only one sprocket hole coincides with the centre-line of a sprocket tooth. To identify this hole and tooth an indentation is made on the sprocket face.

TIMING CHAIN—ADJUSTING.

The amount of free play in the timing chain is controlled by means of a manually operated chain tensioner.

Remove the oil filler cap at the front of the exhaust camshaft cover to gain access to the adjuster screw and locknut. Release the locknut and carefully turn the adjuster screw in a clockwise direction until a strong resistance is felt. Turn the screw back (anticlockwise) three-quarters of a turn to obtain the correct amount of free play in the timing chain and tighten the locknut.

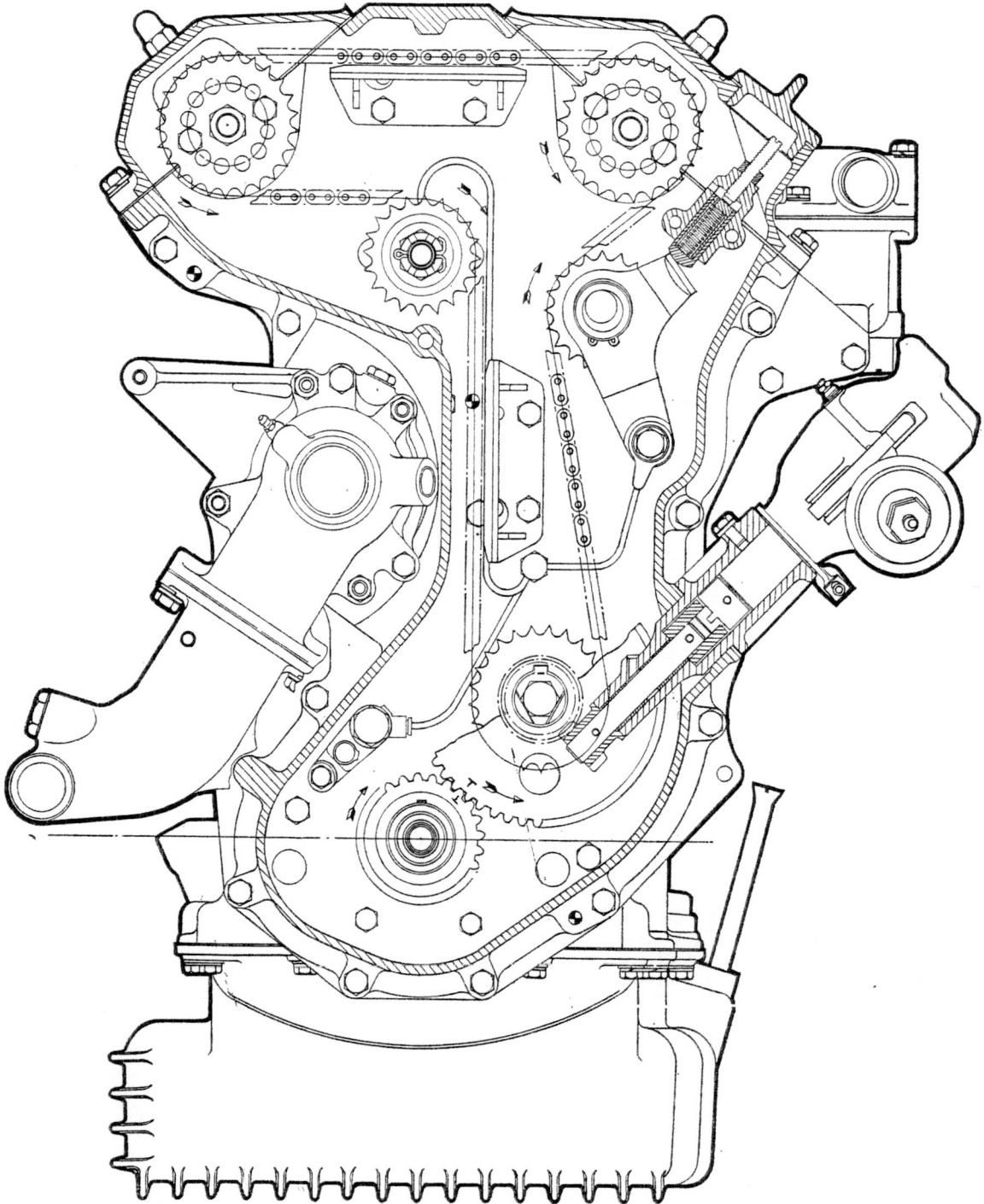

Fig. 7.—The timing chain, tensioner, and distributor drive gear.

PISTON SIZES AND CYLINDER BORES.

When fitting new pistons selective assembly is necessary and to facilitate this the pistons are stamped with identification figures on their crowns. Oversize pistons are marked with the actual oversize dimensions. A piston stamped .020 is only suitable for a bore .020 larger than the standard bore, and similarly pistons with other markings are only suitable for the oversize bore indicated.

After reboring an engine, or whenever fitting pistons differing in size from those removed during dismantling, ensure that the size of the piston fitted is stamped clearly on the top of the cylinder block alongside the appropriate cylinder bore.

Oversize pistons are supplied in the sizes indicated in the following table:—

Piston Marking	Suitable Bore Size
Standard	2.9683 to 2.9698
Oversize:	
+.010	2.9783 to 2.9798
+.020	2.9883 to 2.9898
+.030	2.9983 to 2.9998
+.040	3.0083 to 3.0098

HALF-SPEED SHAFT.

Removal.

Remove the distributor drive gear and housing, and the camshaft covers. Remove the timing chain cover and the timing chain.

Draw off the timing chain driving sprocket with a suitable puller. Remove the sump, oil pump and oil pump drive shaft.

Take out the three setscrews and shakeproof washers which secure the half-speed locating plate

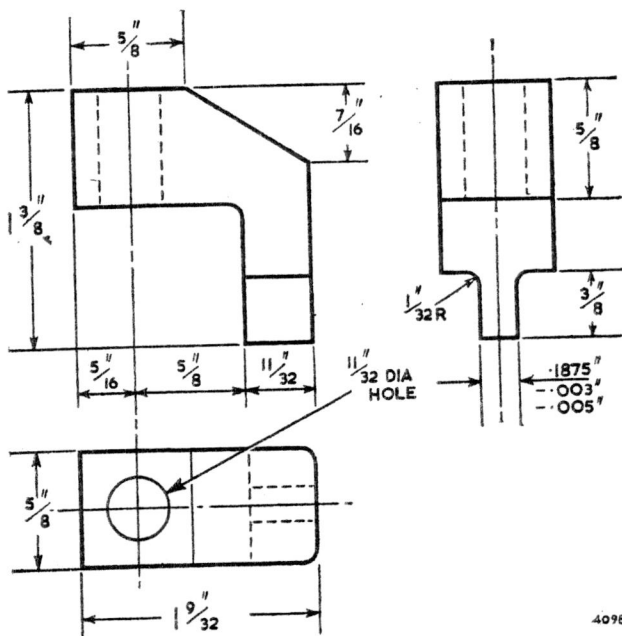

Fig. 8.—A camshaft locking tool dimensions. One tool is required for each camshaft.

and withdraw the half-speed shaft. Note that shims are fitted behind the locating plate to control the half-speed shaft end float.

If the half-speed shaft bearing clearances are excessive new bearings should be fitted. Ensure that the oil holes in the bearings line up with the oil passages in the cylinder block. The bearings must be reamed to give the correct diametrical clearance.

Replacement of the half-speed shaft is a reversal of the above procedure. Adjust the half-speed shaft end float if necessary by increasing or decreasing the thickness of the shims fitted behind the half-speed shaft locating plate.

Turn the engine until No. 4 piston is at T.D.C. on its compression stroke. When the valves on No. 1 cylinder are "rocking" (i.e., exhaust just closing and inlet just opening) No. 4 piston is at the top of its compression stroke. If the engine is set so that the notch in the crankshaft pulley is in line with the projection in the timing chain cover the piston is exactly at T.D.C., giving the correct ignition setting.

Turn the drive gear to the position where the driving slot will be horizontal with the large offset uppermost.

As the gear engages the half-speed shaft the slot will turn in an anti-clockwise direction until it is in the two o'clock position.

Note: If a new or reconditioned oil pump is being fitted it is necessary to remove the half-speed shaft to enable a check of the pump gear end float and "free spin" to be made. After removing the half-speed shaft, mount the pump with drive gear and thrust washer in position and tighten down to the correct torque figure (275 lbs. in.). Check that the shaft rotates freely and that the end float is not excessive. The oil pump must be assembled in the dry condition but lubrication should be used on the oil pump driving gear spindle in the cylinder block. Refit the half-speed shaft.

Pistons and connecting rods are removed from the top of the engine. Connecting rods are **not** marked for identification and the big ends are offset.

GEARBOX

Type: 4-speed with synchromesh on 2nd, 3rd and top. Gear ratios: Top 1.0 to 1; third 1.374 to 1; second 2.214 to 1; first 3.64 to 1; reverse 4.76 to 1. Type of synchronisers: Baulking ring and detent ball. Layshaft bearings: Needle rollers. Mainshaft bearings: Front and rear radial ball, spigot needle roller. Speedometer drive ratio: 5/12.

For details and illustrations see M.G. "MGA" Section.

Note: The "MGA" and "Twin cam" gearboxes are basically the same, with one exception. The mainshaft rear bearing in the extension cover is a bush type with a sliding spline universal joint yoke on the "MGA", while the "Twin cam" assembly has a ball bearing at this point with splined flange secured by a nut and lockwasher and modified mainshaft assembly.

CLUTCH

Make and type: Borg and Beck — 8ARG single dry plate, with hydraulic operation. Plate diameter: 8 inches. Type of hub: Spring cushion. Type of facings: Woven yarn, reinforced. Number of pressure plate springs: 6, coloured light grey. Maximum run-out at flywheel face: .003. Maximum run-out of driven plate: .015. Type of throw-out bearing: Carbon graphite. Pedal adjustment: Clearance master cylinder pushrod to piston, $\frac{1}{32}$ inch. Release lever ratio: 11.7 to 1.

REAR AXLE

Type: B.M.C. "B" type, three-quarter floating. Ratio: 10/43. Crownwheel to pinion backlash: .005 minimum to .007 maximum. Pinion bearing pre-load: 11 to 13 lbs. without oil seal. Differential carrier bearing pre-load: .002 pinch each side. Pinion head washer thickness: .112 to .126 in steps of .002. Pinion bearing pre-load shims: .004 to .012 in steps of .002, plus .020 and .030. Carrier bearing shims: .002, .003, .004, .006 and .010.

See M.G. "MGA" Section for details and illustrations.

Note: The only difference in these two rear axle assemblies is in the brake disc to hub, and caliper attachments on the "Twin cam" as compared to the drum brakes and backplate on the "MGA".

FRONT SUSPENSION

Type: Independent coil spring and wishbone. Castor angle: 4°. Camber angle: 1° positive to $\frac{1}{2}$° negative on full bump. King pin inclination: 9° to $10\frac{1}{2}$° on full bump. Toe-in: Wheels parallel. Coil spring length (free): 9.09 $\pm\frac{1}{16}$ inch. Length: Static 6.60 under 1,193 lbs. load (static). Number of free coils: 7.2. Coil diameter (mean): 3.28.

See M.G. "MGA" Section for details and illustrations.

Note: The only difference between these two suspension units is in the disc brake assemblies as compared with the drum brakes on the "MGA".

STEERING

Type: Rack and pinion. Steering wheel diameter: $16\frac{1}{2}$ inches. Number of turns, lock to lock: $2\frac{2}{3}$.

See M.G. "MGA" Section for details and illustrations.

REAR SUSPENSION

Type: Semi-elliptic leaf springs. Number of spring leaves: 6. Width of leaves: $1\frac{3}{4}$ inches. Thickness of leaves: $\frac{7}{32}$ inch. Working load: 450 lbs. Free camber: 3.60.

BRAKES

Make and type: Dunlop. Disc, front and rear. Disc diameter: 11 inches. Minimum permissible thickness of pads before removal: .250. Maximum permissible disc run-out: .006. Free axial movement of master cylinder pushrod (assembled): .015 to .020.

ELECTRICAL

Type of equipment: Lucas 12 volt, positive earth. Distributor type: Lucas DM2. Coil type: Lucas HA12. Dynamo type: Lucas C39PV2. Field resistance: 6.0 to 6.5 ohms. Brush spring tension: 20 to 25 ozs. Starter type: Lucas 4-brush M35G1. Starter brush spring tension: 30 to 40 ozs. Control box type: Lucas RB106/2.

Control box settings:

Regulator: On open circuit at 68°F. and 1,500 r.p.m. (dynamo): 15.4 to 16.4 volts. For every 18°F. above 68°F. subtract .1 volt. For every 18°F. below 68°F. add .1 volt.

Cut-out cut-in voltage: 12.7 to 13.3. Drop-off voltage: 8.5 to 11.

Reverse current: 5 amps. (maximum).

For wiring diagram, see Figure 9.

Published
The Autocar,
18 July 1958

The radiator grille bears the well-known M.G. octagonal motif. On each side of the bonnet are vents to allow hot air to escape from the engine compartment. Direction indicators are combined with the side lights

Autocar ROAD TESTS

M.G. Twin Cam MGA

OPEN TWO-SEATER

BY producing a high-performance model to partner the successful MGA two-seater, the M.G. Car Company, Ltd., has filled a gap which has been evident to overseas and competition-minded motorists; the new 1,588 c.c. twin overhead camshaft engine will enable the car to compete on equal terms in the 1,300-1,600 c.c. class with Continental-built cars. As described in preceding pages, this engine is a development of the special power unit used in the record-breaking M.G. EX 181.

The new model also has Dunlop 10¾in disc brakes, centre-lock steel wheels and Road Speed tyres, which are not fitted to the standard MGA. The road test car was an open model equipped with hood and side screens and all optionally extra equipment. A coupé version of the car is available.

Powered by the twin carburettor version of the 1½-litre B series engine, the standard MGA coupé is capable of slightly more than 100 m.p.h.; the new 1,600 c.c. unit gives the open car, with hood and side curtains in position, a maximum of 114 m.p.h. It is faster than the 1½-litre car by 1.7sec to 60 m.p.h., and by 15sec to 90 m.p.h.

The engine starts easily and quickly reaches working temperature. It revs freely, and the limit marking on the tachometer is 7,000 r.p.m.; it was taken up to this limit repeatedly during the test.

Engine vibration was noticed at 2,500 and 5,500 r.p.m.; at maximum speed in top gear the tachometer reading was 6,500 r.p.m., and this was held for approximately 5 miles on a level stretch of *autoroute.*

Power builds up noticeably after the engine tops 3,500 r.p.m.; by the time 4,000 r.p.m. is reached it really takes hold and the little car begins to show its potential performance. In first gear it gets very quickly to 30 m.p.h., and a fast change to second gear is needed to avoid exceeding the rev. limit. The comfortable minimum speed in top is 18-20 m.p.h., and in traffic, second and third gears are most used. In open road cruising, 80-90 m.p.h. can be held indefinitely, with plenty in hand for use when required. The car was quite happy at 100 m.p.h. for long stretches on Continental roads, although to maintain high engine speeds has a marked effect on the fuel consumption, of course,

and above 90 m.p.h. the driver has the feeling that the engine is working much harder.

There is a constant, rather obtrusive background of mechanical noise; most of this can be traced to the valve gear, particularly the tappets, which have a recommended clearance of 0.018in, but there is also a "ring" associated with the first stage of the timing gears. Nor can it be said that the engine is smooth or silky. Exhaust-wise, the car is not objectionable, and it can be driven through city traffic without attracting undue attention. This car had a loose silencer baffle. Carburettor intake noise is not noticeable, although only small flame-trap type air cleaners are fitted.

From the performance and maintenance angles, the MGA has an enthusiast's engine. Many of the ancillary units are not easy to reach, as the underbonnet space is filled by the engine itself. The distributor is located below a camshaft housing (it became covered in oil during the test), and the coil is tucked away under the heater trunking. The oil level dipstick would be easier to replace if its containing tube were a little longer. An oil cooler, which is an optional extra, was mounted in front of the radiator, but no oil temperature gauge was supplied.

All maximum speed and acceleration tests were carried

When the side curtains alone are used, the crew can enjoy fresh air motoring with some measure of protection from draughts. The Twin Cam insignia appears beneath the motif on the tail panel

The hood and side curtains are a snug fit and follow closely the contours of the body. There is no exterior door handle. Three large windows at the back of the hood are made of flexible Vybak. Bumper over-riders are standard

out with 100 octane petrol. With this, and Belgian premium petrol (89 research octane rating), the engine tended to "run on" after being switched off. It also used a considerable amount of oil; five pints were added to the sump during one journey of 800 miles, and an overall oil consumption figure of 1,020 m.p.g. was recorded—approximately one quart of oil each time the petrol tank (capacity 10 gallons) was refilled.

Once accustomed to the controls, an experienced driver can get off the mark with very little wheel spin, but it was felt that more suitable gear box ratios would give an even more sparkling getaway, without losing the benefit of easy fast cruising—there is a very noticeable interval between first and second, and between second and third. An owner using the car for circuit racing would, no doubt, prefer a gear box with closer ratios. A 4.55 to 1 axle ratio can be fitted in place of the standard 4.3 to 1 ratio at an extra cost of £10 2s 6d.

Apart from occasional difficulty in selecting first gear when the car is stationary, the gear box is generally pleasant to use. The short, remote control lever has precise movements between the ratios, and very fast changes can be made. One notices a slight difficulty—not uncommon in B-series gear boxes—in getting through the gate transversely, particularly when the gear box is hot. This sometimes makes difficult the change from third into second, and there is a risk that the lever may overshoot into the reverse quadrant. The top of the lever is close to the steering wheel when the latter is set near the facia; it is also well placed in relation to the driving seat. There was no vibration from the transmission, and the axle was silent.

Free from slip during full-bore gear changes, the clutch transmitted the engine power without judder under all conditions. Some adjustment was found necessary to take up pedal movement, but once attended to the need did not recur. Positioning of the pedals is good, although to clear the clutch pedal, the left foot has to be placed beneath it rather than to the left. The accelerator, which is connected to the throttle by a cable, works smoothly, and delicate, progressive control can be achieved.

Among the most delightful features of the MGA are its road-holding and cornering. The manufacturers' well-known motto—Safety Fast—is particularly pertinent to this new model. Changes in road surface have little effect on the manner in which the car sits firmly on the road, and its behaviour on a streaming wet road is equally good, although the tail will swing slightly if the throttle is opened suddenly when cornering. Power can be used judiciously to help the car round a corner, in fact progress on a winding road is all the better if this technique is applied.

There is strong self-centring of the steering, and there is no lost motion to impair its accuracy; from lock to lock requires only 2¾ turns of the wheel, and although the turning circle is greater by 4ft 6in than that of the 1½-litre-engined car, the Twin Cam model can be manœuvred easily in narrow streets.

A slight heaviness in the steering was noticed with the tyres inflated to the normal recommended 18 lb front and 20 lb rear; when pressures were raised by 4 lb sq in, this

heaviness disappeared and the ride was not uncomfortable.

With full load, or with the driver only in the car, there is a satisfactory firmness about the suspension, which reaches an excellent compromise in a car which may be called upon to take the owner to work during the week, and yet be driven in races at the weekend. Stability is first class and there is no heeling-over on corners, although brisk progress is marked by excessive tyre squeal; the latest pattern Road Speed tyres were not fitted to the test car.

The driving position is well suited to most drivers, but a person of small stature would be happier with a higher seat cushion. The steering wheel can be set close to the facia, by a lock-nut and bolt fitting; in this position of adjustment the driver has fingertip control of the horn button and indicator switch. The thin-rimmed wheel is set at an ideal angle for control, being almost vertical; it does not obscure the instruments.

Fitted to the test car were the competition-type seats, which have a padded roll round the edge of the back rest, and long cushion; they proved most comfortable and provided firm support at a good angle. Driver and passenger are well held when cornering fast, and long distances can be covered without fatigue. The proximity of the engine and gear box can bring about an uncomfortably high temperature around the legs and feet; it is probable that owners in hot climates will call for separate fresh air ventilators. On the other hand, the warmth would be appreciated in winter conditions.

All the advantages which this car affords for fast motoring would be wasted if the braking system was not up to the same standards. It is becoming increasingly the practice for 100 m.p.h. cars, whether they are large saloons or agile two-seaters, to be fitted with disc brakes. The Dunlop 10¾in diameter discs fitted to the Twin Cam MGA are adequate to all they are called upon to do in wet or dry. The pedal has a good feel to it, being neither spongy nor too hard, though loads are rather high in normal traffic stops; this is normal with discs, which have no self-servo effect, and is noticeable

A cover encloses the spare wheel, on top of which is strapped the tool kit. The petrol filler has a quick release cap

M.G. Twin Cam
MGA   . . . .

The polished aluminium covers of the camshaft housings dominate the under-bonnet view

when there is no external servo assistance, as in the case of the MGA. Maximum braking brought the car to a standstill all square, and the brakes could be applied hard when the car was being driven fast on wet roads. There was no noticeable increase in pedal travel after 800 miles of fast driving. The front discs did show signs of scoring, which has not been noticed on other cars.

The parking brake is controlled by a fly-off-pattern lever, in which the button is pressed to lock the brake on. The lever is placed between the transmission cover and the driving seat, and the hand falls readily on it.

At night reasonable use can be made of the car's performance, although more powerful head lamps would be appreciated for speeds close to 100 m.p.h.; the dipped beam did not inconvenience oncoming traffic. The Twin Cam MGA is one of the cars which really do require a hand dipper switch. When driving on the open road at night, one needs two left feet to operate the clutch and the foot dipper, for the driver always seems to need to change gear and alter the light setting at the same moment. The positioning of the pedal and switch are such that the changeover cannot be made on the instant.

Facia instruments are well lit, and the switch is fitted with a rheostat. There is a small map light, with a separate switch on the left side of the facia. Self-parking wipers are fitted, and although they are powerful and silent, they are up against an unusual handicap—in heavy rain, water is blown off the bonnet on to the screen and the wipers have difficulty in clearing it. An owner could perhaps prevent this by fitting a shallow Perspex deflector across the bonnet to deflect the air stream up and over the screen.

With the hood and side curtains erected, the car proved weatherproof except at speeds over 90 m.p.h., when wind pressure tended to lift the hood above the middle of the windscreen; rain found its way in there, and also through the scuttle on to the passenger's legs. Although there were gaps between the windscreen frame and the side screens,

rain did not penetrate here. The hood is comparatively simple to erect and can be folded away neatly behind the seat backrests. A plastic bag, secured to the bodywork behind the seats, provided stowage for the side curtains.

With the hood and side curtains erected, a tall driver has no difficulty in getting into or out of the car, and there is ample headroom. In this condition, the occupants find the interior rather warm, and it was not possible to obtain a flow of cool air through the vent above the gear box cover. A heater—part of the extra equipment—proved amply efficient in the moderate temperatures encountered during the test.

Accommodation for maps and small articles is provided by a deep pocket in each door, but as the doors cannot be locked, it is not advisable to stow valuables in these pockets if the car is left unattended. Only the Twin Cam models and the 1½-litre coupé are supplied with a leather-covered facia. A large proportion of the luggage compartment is occupied by the spare wheel and tool kit, and it is not easy to find room for a large suitcase, but a number of small bags and boxes can be stowed away. If coats and soft travelling bags are fitted in carefully, more can be carried than at first appears likely.

The tool kit includes a starting handle and, surprisingly, an old-fashioned, screw-type lifting jack. Two 6-volt batteries are located just forward of the rear axle; to service them the spare wheel and a panel in the floor behind the seats must be removed. The high-pressure electric fuel pump is close to the battery on the right side of the frame. Nine lubrication points require grease gun attention every 1,000 miles.

In the road test of the 1½-litre MGA coupé it was stated in summary that the car was capable of holding its own against more powerful vehicles; this applies even more markedly to the 1,600 c.c. Twin Cam model. The extra performance is matched by the road-holding, steering and brakes, and this car maintains the M.G. tradition of good looks coupled with a very fine performance.

Left: Competition seats, an optional extra, are contoured to give extra support in cornering, and under the thighs. Right: This is a functional facia, with neat, easily read dials. The main switches come quickly to hand. The steering wheel is shown in its nearest adjustment to the facia. The plated support on the left of the windscreen forms a useful grab handle for the passenger

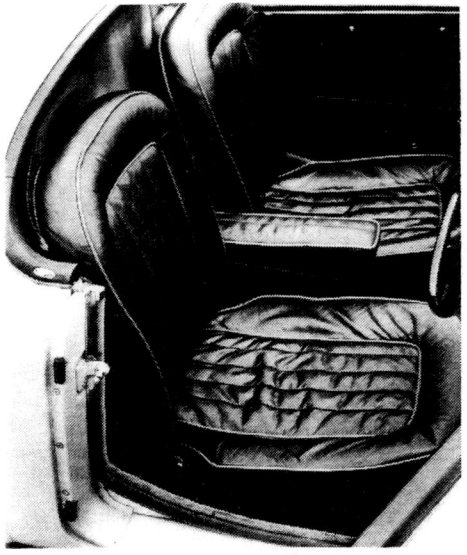

ENGINE

No. of cylinders	...	4 in line
Bore and stroke	...	75.4 x 88.9 mm (2.97 x 3.5in)
Displacement	...	1.588 c.c. (96.91 cu in)
Valve position	...	Twin O.H.C. Hemispherical combustion chamber
Compression ratio	...	9.9 to 1
Max. b.h.p. (nett)	...	108 at 6,700 r.p.m.
Max. b.m.e.p. (nett)	...	163 lb sq in at 4,500 c.p.m.
Max. torque (nett)	...	104 lb ft at 4,500 r.p.m.
Carburettors	...	Twin 1¾ dia S.U. type H.6
Fuel pump	...	S.U. high pressure
Tank capacity	...	10 Imp. gallons (37.8 litres)
Sump capacity	...	12 pints max. (5.7 litres) 7¼ pints min. (3.6 litres)
Oil filter	...	Full flow
Cooling system	...	Pump, fan and thermostat
Battery	...	12 volt, 51 ampère hour

TRANSMISSION

Clutch	...	B and B. 8in dia single dry plate
Gear box	...	4 speeds and reverse, synchromesh on top, 3rd and 2nd. Central lever
Overall ratios	...	Top 4.30; 3rd 5.91; 2nd 9.52; 1st 15.65; reverse 20.47 to 1.
Final drive	...	Hypoid bevel, 4.3 to 1.

CHASSIS

Brakes	...	Dunlop disc. Hydraulic operation. Mechanical calipers for hand brake on rear wheels

Disc dia, pad width	...	10¾in outside dia (2¼ x 1⅜in pads)
Suspension: front	...	Independent, coil springs and wishbones
rear	...	Live axle, half-elliptic leaf springs
Dampers: front	...	Armstrong in unit with wishbone pivots
rear	...	Armstrong lever arm, chassis-mounted
Wheels	...	Dunlop centre-lock steel disc type
Tyre size	...	5.90—15in Dunlop R.S.4
Steering	...	Rack and pinion
Steering wheel	...	16½in dia four spoke
Turns, lock to lock	...	2¼

DIMENSIONS

Wheelbase	...	7ft 10in (239 cm)
Track: front	...	3ft 11.9in (121 cm)
rear	...	4ft 0.87in (124 cm)
Overall length	...	13ft (396 cm)
Overall width	...	4ft 10in (147 cm)
Overall height	...	4ft 2in (127 cm)
Ground clearance	...	6in (15 cm)
Turning circle	...	31ft 4in (9.55 m)
Kerb weight	...	2,156 lb (19¼ cwt) (977 kg)

PERFORMANCE DATA

Top gear m.p.h. per 1,000 r.p.m.	...	17.3
Torque lb ft per cu in engine capacity		1.083
Brake surface area swept by linings		494.8 sq in
Weight distribution (dry)	...	F, 54.6 per cent R, 45.4 per cent

---

M.G. TWIN CAM MGA

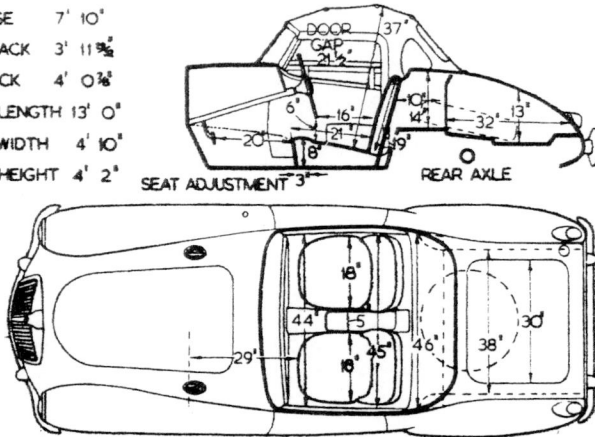

WHEELBASE	7' 10'
FRONT TRACK	3' 11⅞'
REAR TRACK	4' 0⅞'
OVERALL LENGTH	13' 0'
OVERALL WIDTH	4' 10'
OVERALL HEIGHT	4' 2'

Scale ⅛in to 1ft. Driving seat in central position. Cushions uncompressed

━━ DATA ━━

PRICE (basic), with two-seater body, £843. British purchase tax, £422 17s. Total (in Great Britain), £1,265 17s.

Extras:

			£	s	d
Screen washer	..	..	3	0	0
Heater	..	..	18	7	6
Adjustable steering column	..	3	0	0
Oil cooler	..	..	13	10	0
Competition seats	..	9	18	9
Twin horns	..	..	2	1	3

ENGINE: Capacity, 1,588 c.c. (96.91 cu in). Number of cylinders, 4. Bore and stroke, 75.4 × 88.9 mm (2.97 × 3.5in). Valve gear, twin overhead camshafts. Compression ratio, 9.9 to 1. B.H.P. 108 (nett) at 6,700 r.p.m. (B.H.P. per ton laden 96.5). Torque, 104 lb ft at 4,500 r.p.m. M.P.H. per 1,000 r.p.m. in top gear, 17.3.

WEIGHT: (with 5 gals. fuel), 19¼ cwt (2,156 lb). Distribution (per cent): F, 53.9; R, 46.1. Laden as tested, 22¼ cwt (2,506 lb). Lb per c.c. (laden), 1.6.

BRAKES: Type, Dunlop disc. Method of operation, hydraulic. Disc diameter: F, 10¾in; R, 10¾in. Lining swept area: F, 247.4 sq in; R, 247.4 sq in.

TYRES: 5.90—15in. Pressures (lb sq in); F, 18; R, 20 (normal). F, 22; R, 24 (fast driving).

TANK CAPACITY: 10 Imperial gallons. Oil sump, 12 pints. Cooling system, 13½ pints (plus 1 pint if heater fitted).

STEERING: Turning circle, 32ft 6in. Between kerbs, 31ft 4in. Between walls, 33ft 5in. Turns of steering wheel from lock to lock, 2¼.

DIMENSIONS: Wheelbase, 7ft 10in. Track: F, 3ft 11½in; R, 4ft 0¾in. Length (overall), 13ft. Height, 4ft 2in. Width, 4ft 10in. Ground clearance, 6in. Frontal area, 13.8 sq ft (approximately).

ELECTRICAL SYSTEM: 12-volt; 51 ampère-hour battery. Head lamps, Double dip; 50–40 watt bulbs.

SUSPENSION: Front, independent, coil spring and wishbones. Rear, half-elliptic leaf springs with live axle.

━━ PERFORMANCE ━━

ACCELERATION:

Speed Range, Gear Ratios and Time in sec.

M.P.H.	4.30 to 1	5.91 to 1	9.52 to 1	15.65 to 1
10—30	—	—	4.5	3.3
20—40	11.0	7.1	4.5	—
30—50	10.2	7.4	4.9	—
40—60	10.5	7.5	—	—
50—70	11.7	7.6	—	—
60—80	11.7	8.9	—	—
70—90	13.6	—	—	—
80—100	18.7	—	—	—

From rest through gears to:

M.P.H.			sec.
30	..	..	4.3
40	..	..	6.9
50	..	..	9.4
60	..	..	13.3
70	..	..	17.3
80	..	..	22.5
90	..	..	30.0
100	..	..	41.1

Standing quarter mile, 18.6 sec.

MAXIMUM SPEEDS ON GEARS:

Gear			M.P.H.	K.P.H.
Top ..	(mean)		113.5	182.7
	(best)		114.0	183.5
3rd ..	..	..	86	138
2nd ..	..	..	53	85
1st ..	..	..	32	51

TRACTIVE EFFORT:

		Pull (lb per ton)	Equivalent Gradient
Top ..	..	232	1 in 9.6
Third ..	..	315	1 in 7.0
Second ..	..	486	1 in 4.5

SPEEDOMETER CORRECTION: M.P.H.

Car speedometer:	10	20	30	40	50	60	70	80	90	100	110	114
True speed:	11	20	28.5	38.5	48	58	69	80	91	101	112	114

BRAKES (at 30 m.p.h. in neutral)

Pedal load in lb	Retardation	Equivalent stopping distance in ft
25	0.45g	67.2
50	0.62g	48.7
75	0.81g	37.4
90	0.92g	32.8

FUEL CONSUMPTION:

M.P.G. at steady speeds

M.P.H.	Direct Top
30	42.4
40	40.0
50	35.6
60	31.7
70	27.4
80	23.6
90	20.2
100	18.1

Overall fuel consumption for 1,117 miles, 21.8 m.p.g. (12.9 litres per 100 km).

Approximate normal range 18–30 m.p.g. (15.7–9.4 litres per 100 km).

Fuel: Super premium.

TEST CONDITIONS: Weather: overcast, raining. Slight breeze. Acceleration and braking tests on dry surface.

Air temperature, 55–65 deg. F.

Acceleration figures are the means of several runs in opposite directions.

Tractive effort obtained by Tapley meter.

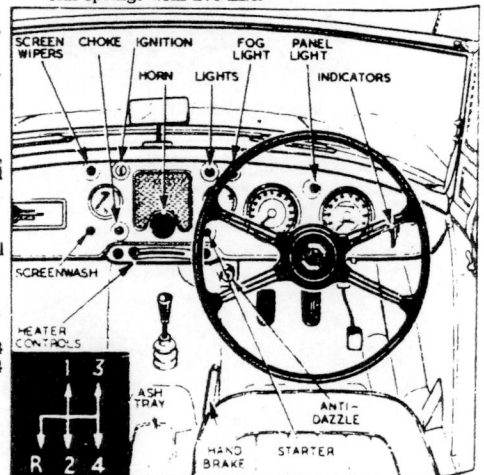

M.G. SERIES MGA

TWO-SEATER, 1956

**First published in
MOTOR TRADER
October 31, 1956**

*Manufacturers: M.G. Car Co., Ltd.,
Abingdon-on-Thames.*

E VOLVED from successive models of sports cars built over the last quarter of a century, and like its original progenitor, the latest M.G. represents a new era of design and construction rather than a new series of models. The M.G. "A" bears but slight resemblance to lineal ancestors of the preceding "T" series, bodywork being restyled in the now conventional form of streamlining, with front wings moulded into the lines of the doors, the bonnet upswept from the near-traditional square M.G. radiator grille, and the rear wings faired off and curved into the luggage boot. This is the first time that this size of M.G. car has been provided with this amenity, and while housing both spare wheel and tool kit, there is space for light luggage items within the boot.

Mechanical developments are evident in that the car is now fitted with the B.M.C. 1½-litre engine unit, which, in its basic form is used in other current Austin and Morris models. The rear axle is also of a standardized pattern, being the B.M.C. "B" type ¾-floating variety with hypoid bevel final drive. These developments mark the general trend of standardization throughout the B.M.C. concern which has led to the fitting of certain variants of basic major units to a number of models in a particular range of vehicles.

Chassis and engine serials are stamped on a plate which is secured to the dash panel beneath the bonnet. The complete symbol of the chassis serial consisting of three letters and two figures, is followed by the usual vehicle serial number. It is most important that all these numbers and letters are quoted in all correspondence with the makers regarding the car, or when ordering spare parts.

Most service operations likely to be encountered can be carried out with the normal range of workshop tools, but a number of special tools have been designed by the makers to speed up and facilitate work which might, without these aids, become lengthy and difficult. Such tools as are considered essential for normal service work are listed in these pages, and are available from the M.G. Car Co., Ltd.

Threads and hexagons are in the main U.N.F.

ENGINE

Mounting

At front, bonded rubber sandwich blocks bolted to angle irons attached to either side of engine front mounting plate. At rear, large circular rubber bush bolted

up with nut and spring washer in annular lug on gearbox extension casing and to chassis frame member.

Removal

Drain oil from gearbox, mark propeller-shaft flanges and disconnect shaft. Mark handbrake cable lever and splined shaft and take off lever, together with reinforcement bracket inside prop. shaft tunnel. Take out seats, frames, floor coverings, floor boards and gearbox cover, with draught excluder and gear-lever knob. Undo speedometer cable drive at gearbox end and remove banjo bolt to release flexible supply pipe from clutch slave cylinder.

Detach bonnet, drain coolant from radiator and disconnect top and bottom water hoses. Remove three securing bolts either side of radiator and take out matrix. Take off carburettors and air cleaners, disconnect rev. indicator drive from cam-

shaft side and undo exhaust pipe at manifold connection, and at steady bracket on rear mounting plate. Disconnect all other pipes, wires and controls to and from engine unit, and place rope around engine and attach lifting tackle; arrange rope so that unit may be lifted slightly and moved forwards, and finally lifted from frame at a sharp angle front uppermost. Take weight of unit on sling, release front mountings and remove rubber blocks. Undo nut, bolt and spring washer to release gearbox from mounting bracket on frame cross-member. Engine-gearbox unit may now be lifted up and manoeuvred out clear of car.

Crankshaft

Three main bearings, thin wall, steel-backed, white metal-lined located by tabs in bearing caps. End float controlled by split thrust washers recessed either side of centre main bearing and retained by

DISTINGUISHING FEATURES—Complete breakaway from the previous conceptions of sports car design, with aerodynamic styling. The traditional radiator grille shape is retained in a modified form

INSTRUMENTS, CONTROLS, GEAR POSITIONS AND BONNET LOCK

1. Wipers.
2. Ignition switch.
3. Lighting switch.
4. Fog lamp switch.
5. Revolution indicator.
6. Panel light switch.
7. Speedometer.
8. Direction indicator.
9. Flasher warning lamp.
10. Main beam warning lamp.
11. Ignition warning lamp.
12. Oil pressure and water temp. gauge.
13. Starter switch.
14. Horn button.
15. De-mister control.
16. Temperature control (blower-pull).
17. Extra air control.
18. Choke control
19. Fuel gauge.
20. Ignition switch.
21. Map light.
22. Bonnet release.
23. Accelerator.
24. Brake.
25. Clutch.
26. Handbrake.
27. Dipper switch.
28. Gear lever.

Inset upper left shows gear positions, and lower left, the bonnet release catch.

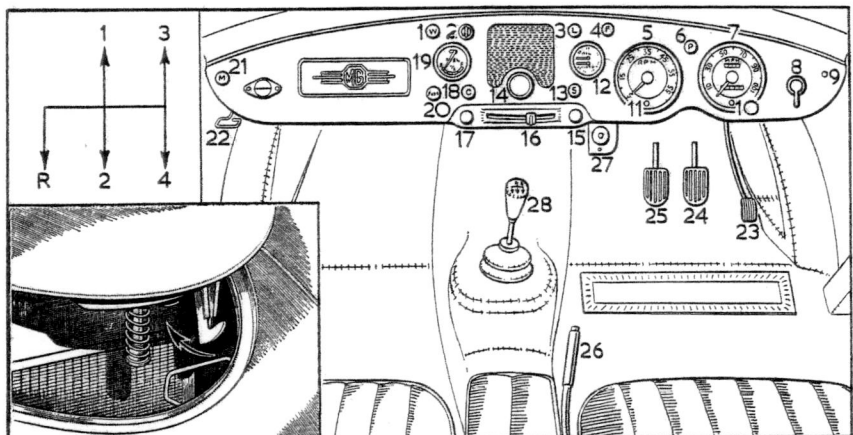

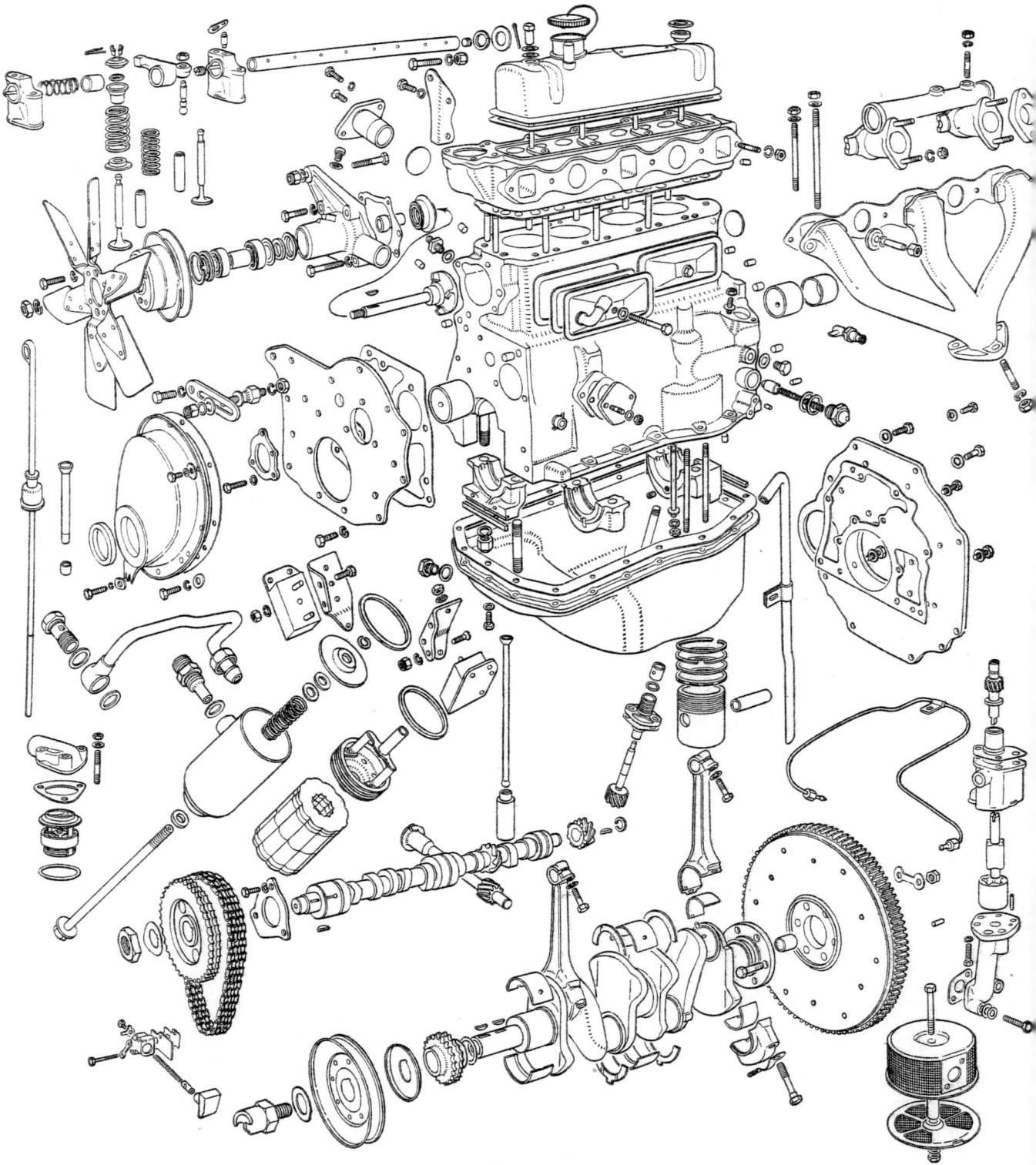

Components of the engine showing the cylinder block and head, timing cover, sump, crankshaft and camshaft, timing gear and piston and con-rod assemblies

SPECIAL TOOLS	Part No.
ENGINE	
Valve spring compressor	18G 271
Water pump assembly tool	18G 60
GEARBOX	
Clutch centraliser	18G 276
Clutch universal gauging fixture ...	18G 99
Dummy layshaft	18G 266
Synchromesh assembly rings ...	18G 222
Synchromesh assembly rings ...	18G 223
REAR AXLE	
Pinion inner race extractor	18G 285
Differential cage bearing extractor...	18G 47C
Adaptors for use with the above ...	18G 47P
Axle pre-load check tool	18G 283
Adaptors for use with the above ...	18G 283A
Rear axle setting tool	18G 191B
Hub nut spanner	18G 267
FRONT AXLE	
Front and rear hub extractors: Plate	18G 304
Bolts	18G 304B
Plug	18G 304J
Steering wheel drawer	18G 310
Steering tie rod spanner female "C"	18G 313
Steering tie rod spanner male ...	18G 312

NUT TIGHTENING TORQUE DATA	lb/ft
Cylinder head nuts	50
Main bearing nuts	70
Connecting rod setscrews	35
Clutch assembly flywheel	50

BALL AND ROLLER BEARING DATA

	Part No.	Int. dia., ext. dia., width (in or mm)	Type
ENGINE			
Water pump drive ...	2A 457	$\frac{1}{2}\times1\frac{5}{16}\times\frac{3}{8}$in	B
GEARBOX			
Layshaft:			
rear end ...	3H 2864	3×15.8 mm	N/R
Front end (outer) ...	3H 2864	3×15.8 mm	N/R
Front end (inner) ...	3H 2865	3×15.8 mm	N/R
1st motion shaft ...	6K 885	$1\frac{3}{8}\times3\times\frac{11}{16}$in	B
1st motion shaft ...	6K 892	3×28 mm	N/R
3rd motion shaft centre	6K 528	$1\frac{1}{8}\times2\frac{13}{16}\times\frac{13}{16}$in	B
REAR AXLE			
Differential (side) ...	2K 8938	40×18×8	B
Pinion (inner)	6K 287	1.750×2.8593×.9375 in	TR
Pinion (outer)	2A 7213	$1\times2\frac{1}{2}\times\frac{5}{8}$ in	TR
Rear wheel hubs ...	2K 7477	40×80×23	B
FRONT AXLE			
Front wheel hub (inner)	ACF 4002	30×72×19	B
Front wheel hub (outer)	ACF 4000	20×52×15	B

GENERAL DATA	
Wheelbase	7ft 10in
Track: front (disc wheels)	3ft $11\frac{1}{2}$in
(wire wheels)	3ft $11\frac{7}{8}$in
rear	4ft $0\frac{3}{4}$in
Turning circle	28ft 0in
Ground clearance	6in
Tyre size: front	5.60—15
rear	5.60—15
Overall length	13ft 0in
Overall width	4ft 10in
Overall height	4ft 2in
Weight (kerb)...	1988lb

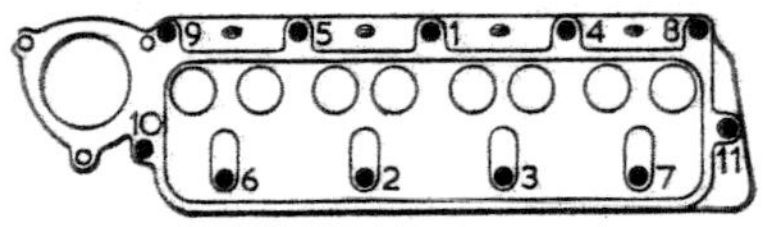

Diagram showing order of tightening cylinder head nuts. See also "Nut Tightening Torque Data"

tabs in cap. Fit with oil grooves to crankshaft. No hand-fitting permissible. Bearings may not be changed without removal of shaft. Flywheel spigot mounted and flange bolted to crankshaft by six bolts and nuts. Spigot bush, renewable, pressed into crankshaft end, shrunk-on starter ring gear fitted. Timing sprocket keyed to front end of crankshaft by Woodruff key; aligning shim abuts against inner boss of sprocket. Renewable felt oil seal fitted into timing case cover. Dynamo and water pump drive pulley keyed to crankshaft by outer of two Woodruff keys, retained by starter dog screw. Sump sealing effected by composition gasket around flange and one square section seal at rear, along bottom of rear main bearing cap which forms lower half of collecting ring around oil return thread on crankshaft. A similar seal is fitted to the front main bearing cap.

Connecting Rods

Big ends offset, thin wall bearings, steel-backed, white metal-liners located by tabs in caps and connecting rod. No hand fitting permissible. H-section rod split diagonally for removal upwards through cylinder bore. Oil bleed hole on longer side of bearing facing away from camshaft. Gudgeon pin bolt clamped in split small ends, clamp bolts towards camshaft.

Pistons

Aluminium alloy, dished crown, split skirted. When assembling, correct clearance of piston in bore measured at right angles to gudegon pin on piston skirt is .0017-.0023in. Fit with split skirt to non-thrust, camshaft side.

Top compression ring plain, second and third rings taper faced. When being assembled taper faced rings must be fitted with side marked "T" (top), uppermost. All rings including scraper fitted above gudgeon pin. Big ends will pass through bores, remove and assemble through top.

Camshaft

Double roller endless chain drive. Camshaft sprocket keyed by Woodruff key to shaft and retained by lock tab and nut. Spring loaded slipper type tensioner fitted, provides automatic take up of slack in chain. Camshaft runs in three white metal-lined steel-backed bearing shells pressed into block. Endfloat control on front bearing. Dot punch marks indicate correct timing and must be together when crankshaft keyway is at T.D.C. and camshaft keyway at 1 o'clock.

Valves

Overhead non-interchangeable. Inlet larger than exhaust, split cone cotter fixing retained by spring clips. Rubber sealing rings with retainers on valve stems below collars. Valve guides plain, no shoulder, non-interchangeable, exhaust guides counterbored at bottom, and both types are countersunk at top. Guides should be pressed or driven in from top until they project $\frac{3}{8}$in from machined surface of valve spring seat.

Tappets and Rockers

Shouldered barrel tappets sliding direct in crankcase. Access through opening in side. Bushed rockers all interchangeable, on shaft carried in four pillars, shaft located by stud and retained by lock plate in No. 4 pillar which is drilled for oil feed through drillings in head and cylinder block. Pair of rockers for each cylinder positioned on either side of pillar, located by separating springs between rockers of adjacent cylinders.

Pushrods can be removed after adjustment has been slackened right off. Inner rockers can be pulled aside against separating springs. End rockers may be taken off after removal of split pin, plain washer and double coil spring washer. Note: Valve springs must be compressed before rockers can be pulled aside.

Lubrication

Hobourn-Eaton eccentric rotor pump flange bolted in recess at rear of cylinder block and driven by slotted shaft from skew gear at rear end of camshaft. Pump may be removed after taking off sump and pick-up strainer and three securing nuts. Pump body bolts to be undone after removal of assembly from engine to dismantle pump. Cylindrical gauze intake strainer in sump.

ENGINE DATA	
General	
Type	BP 15 GB
No. of cylinders	4
Bore x stroke: mm ...	73.025×89
in	2.875×3.50
Capacity: c.c.	1489
cu in	90.88
R.A.C. rated h.p.	13.2
B.M.E.P. at r.p.m. ...	128.8 lb/sq in @ 3500
Max. torque at r.p.m. ...	77.4 lb/ft @ 3500
Compression ratio	8.3:1

CRANKSHAFT AND CON. RODS

	Main Bearings	Crankpins
Diameter ...	2.000in	1.875in
Length ...	1.375in	1.000in
Running clearance:		
main bearings		.0005-.002in
big ends		.0001-.0016in
End float: main bearings ...		.002-.003in
big ends ...		.008-.012in
Undersizes		.010, .020, .030, .040
Con. rod centres		6.50in
No. of teeth on starter ring gear/pinion		120/9

PISTONS AND RINGS	
Clearance (skirt): bottom ...	.0017-.0023in
top ...	.0035-.0042in
Oversizes ...	.010, .020, .030, .040in
Weight without rings or pin	10 oz (approx.)
Gudgeon pin: diameter ...	.6869-6971in
fit in piston	.0001-.00035in Hand push @ 68° F
fit in con. rod	clamped

	Compression	Oil Control
No. of rings ...	3	1
Gap ...	.008-.013in	.008-.013in
Side clearance in grooves ...	.0015-.0035in	.0016-.0036in
Width of rings ...	.111-.118in	.1552-.1562in

CAMSHAFT

	Front	Centre	Rear
Bearing journal: diameter	1.788-1.789in	1.728-1.729in	1.622-1.623in
length	$1\frac{21}{32}$in	$1\frac{3}{32}$in	$\frac{13}{16}$in
Bearing clearance ...	.001-.002in		
End float ...	.003-.007in		
Timing chain: pitch	$\frac{3}{8}$in		
No. of links ...	52		

VALVES

	Inlet	Exhaust
Head diameter	$1\frac{1}{2}$in	$1\frac{9}{32}$in
Stem diameter	$\frac{11}{32}$in	$\frac{11}{32}$in
Face angle	45°	45°
	Inner	**Outer**
Spring length:		
free	$1\frac{31}{32}$in	$2\frac{3}{64}$in
fitted	$1\frac{7}{16}$in	$1\frac{9}{16}$in
load (valve open) ...	50lb	105lb

Cooling System

Pump and fan, thermostat in water outlet port on cylinder head. Pump spindle runs in two ball bearings and has renewable seal. Adjust fan belt until there is ½in play either way in vertical run of belt.

TRANSMISSION

Clutch

Borg and Beck single dry plate, hydraulically operated. Sintered carbon thrust release bearing. Operating cylinder paired with brake master cylinder and mounted on chassis frame. Slave cylinder bolted to bell-housing and connected to clutch operating lever. Only adjustment provided is between master cylinder pushrod and piston, when clutch pedal is released. Adjust pushrod after slackening locknut to give ³⁄₃₂in clearance. Access to clutch obtained after removal of power unit and gearbox.

Gearbox

Four-speed, synchromesh on 2nd, 3rd and top speeds, sliding spur type gears on 1st and reverse. Remote control by short central lever.

To Remove Gearbox

Remove engine/gearbox unit as detailed in engine section, and take off starter motor. Unscrew bolts and nuts securing bell-housing and exhaust pipe brackets and withdraw gearbox and rear extension from engine, taking care to keep gearbox flange parallel with crankcase face until 1st motion shaft is clear of clutch.

To Dismantle Gearbox

Extract dipstick, drain plug and speedometer drive; unscrew nuts and remove gear lever remote control tower and joint washer. Unscrew and remove six bolts and take off rear extension cover and joint washer. Remove interlock arm and

Parts of the gearbox, showing gear trains, selector mechanism and gear-case

bracket. Remove one nut and seven setscrews and take off rear extension and manœuvre remote control shaft selector lever from selectors. Unscrew three countersunk screws and seven hexagon head setscrews and take off gearbox cover and overshoot stop. Cut locking wire and unscrew three change speed fork setscrews. Unscrew two setscrews and remove shifter shaft locating block with shifter shafts; note two dowels in block, preserve three selector balls and springs. Withdraw forks from box in following order: Reverse, top and third, first and second. Unscrew clutch lever pivot nut, screw out pivot bolt and remove lever with thrust bearing. Unscrew nuts and take off gearbox front cover, noting bearing shims between cover and bearing. Tap out layshaft allowing cluster to rest in bottom of box. Take out retaining setscrew and remove reverse shaft and gear; withdraw mainshaft assembly to rear. Withdraw first motion shaft assembly complete with 18 spigot needle rollers using tool No. 18G266 if necessary. Lift out layshaft cluster and two thrust washers.

To dismantle rear extension, release front and rear selector levers from the remote control shaft by taking out clamping screws and sliding levers from rod. Extract keys from shaft and take out remote control shaft from extension.

To dismantle mainshaft assembly, remove items in following order: baulk ring, synchro sleeve and hub; second baulk ring. If and when synchro sleeve is removed from its hub, care should be taken to preserve three locating balls and springs. Press down third speed thrust washer locating peg, rotate splined washer to line up with those on shaft and remove washer. Take off 3rd speed gear and brass bush, also thrust washer to release 2nd speed gear, bush and baulk ring. Remove thrust washer from splined shaft and take off 2nd speed gear and hub. Take off rear retaining nut, washer and speedo drive gear and key together with distance-piece, from shaft. Take off bearing and its housing. Extract one

circlip from laygear, push out bearing and distance tube assemblies (three needle races, two distance tubes equally spaced).

To Assemble Gearbox

Reverse procedure of dismantling, noting following points: Layshaft—fit circlip to innermost groove in gear, hold shaft vertically in vice, assemble a roller bearing on shaft against vice jaws and slide gear over shaft and bearing with largest gear downwards. Remove shaft from vice and push bearing into gear against circlip. Fit end roller bearing assembly and retaining circlip. Slide distance tube into other end of gear followed by other end bearing and circlip.

Mainshaft

Assemble from front, locate internally splined thrust washer on front end of splines. Push longer brass bush up to splines, dogs frontwards. Oil hole in bush must register with oil hole in shaft. Cutaway at front end of second (shorter) bush must line up with locating peg in shaft when dogs of two bushes and washer are engaged. Fit 2nd speed baulk ring and gear on to bush plain side frontwards. Slide on brass thrust washer and shorter brass bush, lugs locating in thrust washers. Fit on 3rd speed gear, cone frontwards. Insert spring and plunger into hole in shaft, threading on front thrust washer depressing plunger through hole in 3rd gear cone, and turn washer to lock. Fit three springs and balls to top/3rd synchro assembly and slide into position with two baulk rings. Following items to be assembled from rear: three balls and springs in second gear bush followed by synchro-hub; first speed gear, synchro-hub and baulk ring to splines on shaft. Press rear bearings into housing and fit to shaft. Push on distance sleeve, speedo drive gear and key, lock washer and nut. Assemble rear extension and fit to gearbox locating control shaft front selector lever in shifter rod selectors. Replace interlock arm on rear extension side cover flange and refit cover.

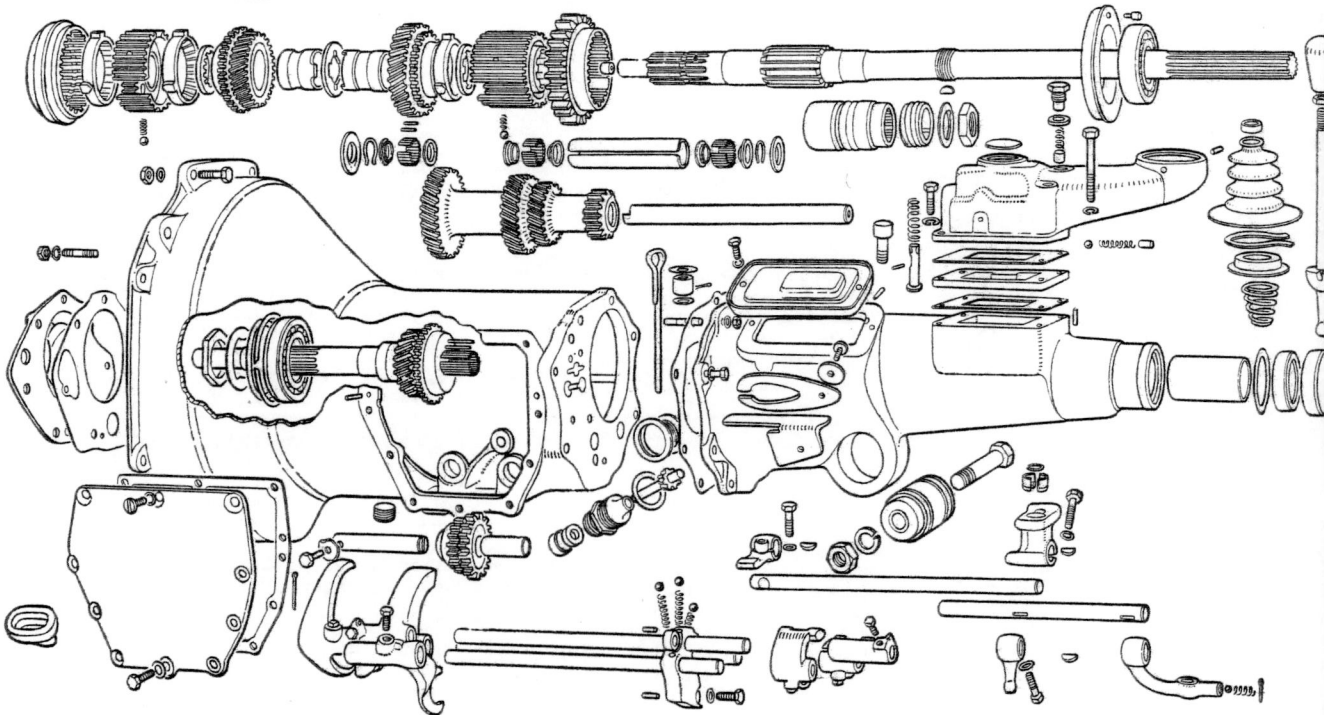

Replace laygear in box complete with thrust washers, assemble and replace 1st motion shaft together with 18 spigot needle rollers. Insert 3rd motion shaft from rear and push home shaft, rear bearing and housing, and enter spigot in needle roller race of 1st motion shaft. Fit layshaft and thrust washers, lining up cutaway portion of shaft end with locating groove in front cover. Fit reverse gear and shaft, front end cover and bearing shims, clutch lever and fork. Fit selectors to shifter shaft rear ends together with locating block, balls and springs. Insert shafts followed by selector forks. Refit rear extension, locate change speed gate and fit side cover; screw in speedometer drive gear, plugs and breather.

Propeller-shaft

Hardy-Spicer needle roller bearing universal joints. Reverse spline type sliding joint fitted between gearbox and front universal joint flange. Nipples provided for lubrication of joints.

Rear Axle

Three-quarter floating, hypoid bevel drive. Rear cover welded to banjo housing.

To remove axle from car, lift rear of car and remove wheels, disconnect propeller shaft rear end and shock absorbers. Take weight of axle on jack and remove brake pipe lines from back plates. Remove split pin and clevis pin securing brake cables to each operating lever. Remove small nut and Phillips screw securing handbrake cable clip to axle; take off brake balance lever from pivot on casing. Release exhaust pipe from manifold and supporting brackets and remove pipe assembly complete. Remove rear and then front bolts of spring anchorages and take out "U" bolts. Draw out axle to rear clear of car.

Half-shafts (interchangeable) upset at outer ends to form flanges which register on wheel studs on hub flanges. Hubs run on ball bearings retained on axle tube ends by nuts with tab-washers. Lipped oil seal in hub behind bearing (lip to bearing), and spacer washer is fitted on outer side of bearing. If shaft is withdrawn, note paper gasket behind flange.

Bevel pinion shaft runs in taper roller bearings. Outer races pressed into final drive housing. Distance-piece between inner races, which are nipped up by driving flange nut. Shims between distance-piece and front bearing (.004-.012in available) regulate preload on bearings, which should give 14-16lb/in drag with oil seal fitted. No adjustment for pinion mesh without special tools and graded distance pieces.

Crown wheel spigoted on one-piece differential cage and retained by six setscrews. Differential side bevel gears run directly in cage, planet pinions have spherical washers.

Differential assembly carried in semithrust ball bearings in split housings. Thrust side of bearings must face outwards. Shims between differential cage and inner races of bearings for mesh adjustment. Adjust so that the crown wheel is just free without play, and backlash is as etched crown wheel (usually .006-.009in), then add shims to offside bearing to give .002in total preload. Differential assembly should then be light push fit in housing. Backlash must be not less than .006in

CHASSIS

Brakes

Lockheed hydraulic. Two leading shoe front brakes with separate cylinder to each shoe. Rear brakes have single floating cylinder incorporating bell-crank for handbrake operation.

Micram adjuster on each wheel cylinder, with slotted head reached through holes in drum and wheel, holes now sealed by rubber plugs. Turn adjuster clockwise until shoe touches drum, then back off one notch. Note two adjusters on each front wheel.

Handbrake cable has adjusting nut on screwed end of cable located beneath car in centre. Brake shoes must be adjusted before cable is taken up. Make sure that cable nut is properly bedded on trunnion after adjustment.

Rear Springs

Semi-elliptic. Loose rubber shackle and anchorage bushes (all interchangeable). Shackle pins and anchorage bolts shouldered, tighten fully. Anchorage bolts have heads drilled for peg spanner, and are inserted from inner side of bracket. **Shackle pins and anchorage bolts must be tightened with car in static laden position.**

Front Suspension

Independent, coil springs and double wishbone links. Inner ends of upper links pivot on shock absorbers. Inner ends of lower links rubber bushed. Outer ends of both links pivot in bronze bushes in pivot lugs, which are threaded on to king pins. Near side king pin and stub axle have left-hand threads.

If suspension is to be dismantled, jack up chassis until front wheels are just clear of ground, then jack up separately under each spring pad until upper link is clear of rebound rubber. Disconnect track rods by slackening locknuts and screwing rods out of outer ball sockets. Disconnect brake hoses from chassis unions, and take out outer pivot bolts, when stub axle, king pin and pivot lug assembly can be removed. Release jacks under springs, press down lower links and take out springs. Dismantle lower links and remove from inner pivots. Rubber bush assemblies are similar to those on rear spring shackles. Upper links are removed with shock absorbers (two setscrews, and two bolts inserted from below through spring abutment—note flats on bolt heads to register with edge of spring locating plate, through which bolts pass).

King pins pressed downwards into stub axle and located by steering arms. Pivot lugs screw on to king pins, which are waisted at centre of top and bottom threads to clear pivot bolts. When reassembling make sure that stub axle swivels fully.

Outer pivot bearings consist of bush in lug, cut away to clear king pin, and distance-piece, which is clamped up by bolt with link, thrust washers and seal retainers, and works in bush. Distance-piece should stand proud of lug at each end to give .008-.013in end play.

Hubs run on ball bearings with distance-piece between inner races. Lipped oil seal pressed into back of each hub bears on chamfered collar behind inner race of inner bearing. Bearings

retained on stub axles by castellated nuts. Tighten fully.

Outer steering ball joints are sealed side plug type, serviced as assembly.

Adjust track (wheels parallel) by screwing track rods in outer ball sockets. Both track rods must be of equal length. Check distance from flat on rod to locknut.

Steering Gear

Rack and pinion. Inner ends of short track rod attached to ends of rack by ball joints covered by concertina gaiters and lubricated from steering gear. Track rods interchangeable. Upper section of steering column connected to universal joint fixed to column tube.

CHASSIS DATA

CLUTCH

Make	...	Borg & Beck
Type...	...	sdp A6-G
Springs: no.	...	6
colour	...	Black/yellow
free length	...	2.16in
Centre springs: no.	...	6
colour	...	White/lt. green
Linings: thickness	...	.120-.130in
dia. ext.	...	8in ± $\frac{1}{32}$in
dia. int.	...	5$\frac{3}{4}$in ± .010 .000 } in

GEARBOX

Type...	...	Synchromesh
No. of forward speeds	...	4
Final ratios: 1st	...	15.652 : 1
2nd	...	9.520 : 1
3rd	...	5.908 : 1
4th	...	4.3 : 1
Rev...	...	20.468 : 1

PROPELLER-SHAFT

Make	...	Hardy Spicer
Type...	...	Needle roller bearing U.J.

FINAL DRIVE

Type...	...	$\frac{3}{4}$-floating hypoid
Crownwheel/bevel pinion teeth	...	10/43 std; 9/41 opt.

BRAKES

Type...	...	Lockheed hydraulic
Drum diameter	...	10in
Lining: length	...	9.6 in
width	...	1.72in
thickness	...	.200in
No. of rivets per shoe	...	12

SPRINGS

	Front	Rear
Length (eye centres, laden)	—	
Coil diameter (mean)	3.238in	
Width	—	1$\frac{3}{4}$in
Wire diameter	.498in	—
No. of leaves or coils	7.5	6
Free camber (length, coil)	9.28 ± $\frac{1}{16}$in	3.60in
Loaded camber (length, coil) at load	6.65 ± $\frac{1}{2}$ @ 905lb	405lb @

SHOCK ABSORBERS

Make	...	Armstrong
Type...	...	Piston
Service	...	Top up

STEERING BOX

Make	...	Morris B.M.C.
Type...	...	Rack and pinion
Adjustments:		
rack end float	...	shims on damper
pinion end float	...	thrust washer
mesh	...	shims on damper

FRONT-END SERVICE DATA

Castor	...	4°
Camber	...	1° pos to $\frac{1}{2}$° neg
King pin inclination	...	9° to 10$\frac{1}{2}$°
Toe-in	...	Nil
No. of turns lock to lock	...	2$\frac{3}{4}$
Adjustments: castor		—
camber		
toe-in		screwed tie rod ends

Parts of the front suspension, steering and rear axle assemblies

TUNE-UP DATA

Firing order	1-3-4-2	gap ...	.019-.021in
Tappet clearance (hot):		Carburetter: make ...	S.U. (twin)
inlet	.017in	type ...	H.4 (semi-d.d.)
exhaust	.017in	Settings: Choke ...	1½in
for timing	.021in	Needles ...	G.S.
Valve timing:		Jet ...	.090in
inlet opens	16° B.T.D.C.	Piston spring ...	Red
inlet closes	56° A.B.D.C.	Air cleaner: make ...	Vokes
exhaust opens	51° B.B.D.C.	type ...	Oil wet
exhaust closes	21° A.T.D.C.	Fuel pump: make ...	S.U.
Standard ignition timing ...	7° B.T.D.C.	type ...	Electric
Location of timing marks...	marked chain wheels	Delivery test ...	10 gal/hr
Plugs: make	Champion	Suction lift ...	33in
type size	N.A.8 14 mm	Output lift ...	48in

BULBS

Component	Lucas No.	Voltage	Wattage	Cap					
					Side/flasher	380	12	21/6	S.B.C.
					Stop/flasher	380	12	21/6	S.B.C.
					Map	222	12	4	M.C.C.
Headlamp:					Panel	987	12	2.2	M.E.S.
R.H.D.	354	12	42/36	Prefocus	Ignition	987	12	2.2	M.E.S.
Export	370	12	45/40	Prefocus	Main beam	987	12	2.2	M.E.S.
Fog lamp	323	12	48	Prefocus	Flasher	987	12	2.2	M.E.S.
No. plate	222	12	4	M.C.C.					

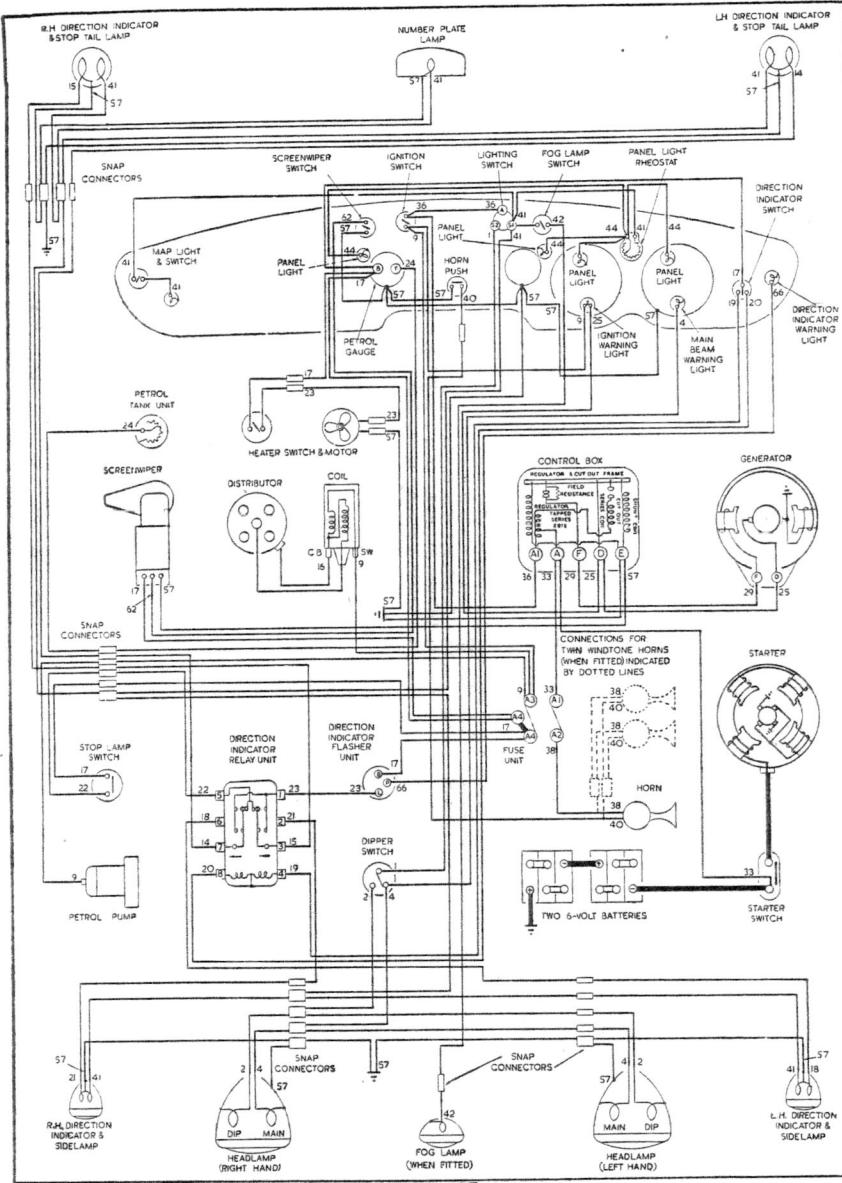

COLOUR CODE

1 BLUE	9 WHITE	17 GREEN	25 YELLOW	33 BROWN	41 RED	49 PURPLE	57 BLACK
2 BLUE WITH RED	10 WHITE WITH RED	18 GREEN WITH RED	26 YELLOW WITH RED	34 BROWN WITH RED	42 RED WITH YELLOW	50 PURPLE WITH RED	58 BLACK WITH RED
3 BLUE WITH YELLOW	11 WHITE WITH YELLOW	19 GREEN WITH YELLOW	27 YELLOW WITH BLUE	35 BROWN WITH YELLOW	43 RED WITH WHITE	51 PURPLE WITH YELLOW	59 BLACK WITH YELLOW
4 BLUE WITH WHITE	12 WHITE WITH BLUE	20 GREEN WITH BLUE	28 YELLOW WITH WHITE	36 BROWN WITH BLUE	44 RED WITH BLUE	52 PURPLE WITH BLUE	60 BLACK WITH BLUE
5 BLUE WITH GREEN	13 WHITE WITH GREEN	21 GREEN WITH WHITE	29 YELLOW WITH GREEN	37 BROWN WITH WHITE	45 RED WITH GREEN	53 PURPLE WITH WHITE	61 BLACK WITH GREEN
6 BLUE WITH PURPLE	14 WHITE WITH PURPLE	22 GREEN WITH PURPLE	30 YELLOW WITH PURPLE	38 BROWN WITH PURPLE	46 RED WITH PURPLE	54 PURPLE WITH GREEN	62 BLACK WITH PURPLE
7 BLUE WITH BROWN	15 WHITE WITH BROWN	23 GREEN WITH BROWN	31 YELLOW WITH BROWN	39 BROWN WITH PURPLE	47 RED WITH BROWN	55 PURPLE WITH BROWN	63 BLACK WITH BROWN
8 BLUE WITH BLACK	16	24	32 YELLOW WITH BLACK	40 BROWN WITH BLACK	48 RED WITH BLACK	56	64

Wiring Diagram by permission of Joseph Lucas Ltd.

LUCAS EQUIPMENT AND TEST DATA

BATTERY
Model SG9E
Capacity at 10-hour rate: 51 ampere-hour
Capacity at 20-hour rate: 58 ampere-hour

Specific Gravity	Climates under 90°F	Climates over 90°F
Fully charged	1.270-1.290	1.210-1.230
Half discharged	1.190-1.210	1.130-1.150
Completely discharged	1.110-1.130	1.050-1.070

GENERATOR
Model C39 PV-2   Part No. 22258
2 pole, 2 brush shunt wound, ventilated, compensated voltage control. Connection: Yellow lead to main D terminal; yellow lead with green tracer to field F terminal: cross connections will cause serious damage to regulator in control box. Rotation: clockwise (driving end). Brush tension: 22-25 oz. Field resistance: 6.1 ohms. Maximum output 19 amps at 1900-2150 r.p.m. at 13.5 volts. Change brushes when worn to 11/32in.

CONTROL BOX
Model RB 106-2   Part No. 37182
Cut-out: Cut-in voltage 12.7-13.3 volts
Drop-off voltage: 8.5-11.0 volts

Voltage regulator:	Open-circuit settings at:
10°C (50°F)	15.9-16.5 volts
20°C (68°F)	15.6-16.2 volts
30°C (86°F)	15.3-15.9 volts
40°C (104°F)	15.0-15.6 volts

STARTING MOTOR
Model M35G-1   Part No. 25022
4 brush, 4-pole series-parallel field. Rotation: Clockwise (driving end). Drive: "S.B." type, inboard. Brush tension: 15-25 oz. Lock torque: 9.3 lb/ft with 370-390 amps at 7.7 to 7.3 volts. Torque at 1000 r.p.m. (starter): 4.9 lb/ft with 230-250 amps at 9.3-8.9 volts. Change brushes when worn to 5/16in.

DISTRIBUTOR
Model DM2P4   Part No. 40488 & 40510
Contact breaker spring tension: 18-24oz
Contact breaker setting: 0.014-0.016in
Contacts closed period: 60° ± 3°
Contact set Nos.: 420196 & 423153 respectively
Condenser capacity: 0.18-0.23mf
Minimum insulation: 3 megohms
Rotation (drive end): clockwise
Centrifugal advance commences @ 125-275 r.p.m.
Max. centrifugal advance at 11°-13° at 975 r.p.m.
Centrifugal advance springs 416 111/S
Vacuum advance commences at 6in Hg
Max. vacuum advance at 9°-11° with 20in Hg.

IGNITION COIL
Model HA12   Part No. 45054
Primary resistance: 3.6
Running current at 1000 r.p.m.: 1.4

WINDSCREEN WIPER
Model DR2   Part No. 75297
Total current consumption: 2.3-3.4 amp
Field current: 0.9 amp

HORNS
Model WT 618   Part No. 69046 low note
                         69047 high note
Type: Windtone
Current consumption: 6-7 amp, each horn

FLASHER UNIT
Model FL3   Part No. 35003
Rate of flashing 60-120 flashes per minute
Light period/dark period ratio 50/50 ± 10%

Model SF6   Part No. 033239
Fuse ratings: 35 amp and 35 amp

Component	Model	Part No.
Flasher relay	DB 10	33117
Lamps: Head R.H.D. ...	F 700	51344
L.H.D. ...	F 700	51345
Export Europe ...	F 700	51346
Export France ...	F 700	51411
Fog	SFT 576	55128D (optional)
No. plate illumination ...	467-2	53093
Side and flasher ...	539	52236
Stop tail and flasher ...	549	53330
Map light cover ...	534	573914
Map light glass ...		573915
Flasher warning ...	WL 13	38132
Switches:		
Dipper	FS 22-1	31284
Direction indicator ...	TPS 1	31250
Fog lamp	PS 7	31515
Horn push	HP 19	76205
Ignition	S 45	31449
Lighting	PPG 1	31251
Map	PS 7	31515
Panel light rheostat ...	CHR 1	78311
Starter push ...	ST 19-2	76423
Stop light	HL 2	31082
Wiper	PS 7	31515

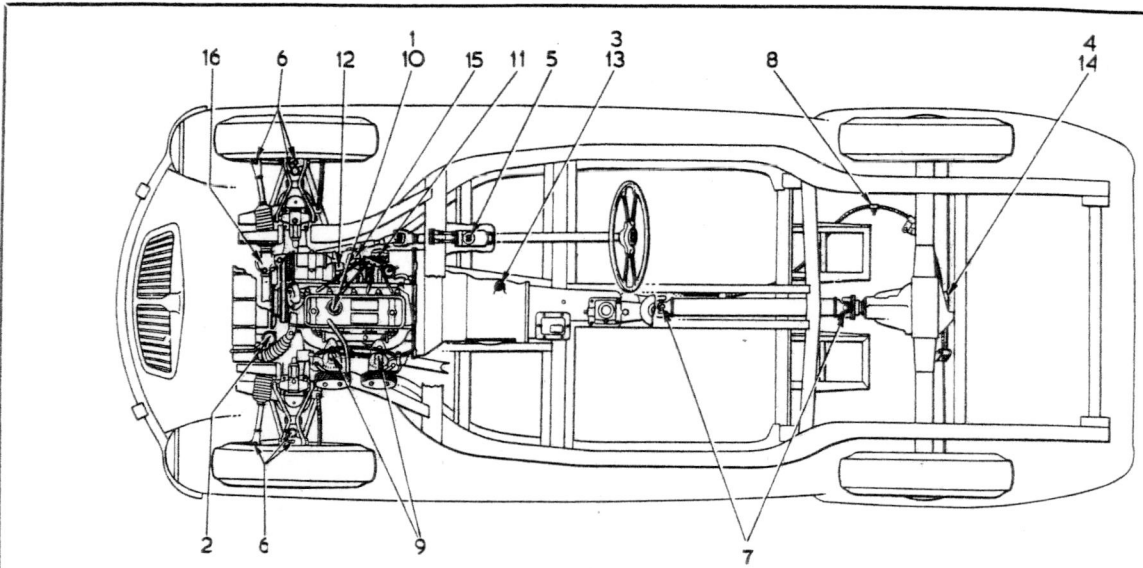

KEY TO MAINTENANCE DIAGRAM

EVERY 250 MILES

1. Engine sump } Top up
2. Radiator

EVERY 1,000 MILES

3. Gearbox
4. Rear axle } Top up
5. Brake and clutch master cylinder
6. Steering joints
7. Propeller-shaft universal joints } Grease gun
8. Handbrake cable
9. Carburettor suction chambers—oilcan

EVERY 3,000 MILES

10. Engine sump—Drain and refill
11. Distributor—Oil spindle and advance mechanism, contact breaker pivot, grease cam
12. Dynamo—Oil end bearing

EVERY 6,000 MILES

13. Gearbox } Drain and refill
14. Rear axle
15. External oil filter—Renew

EVERY 12,000 MILES

16. Steering gearbox—Oil gun

DRAINING POINTS

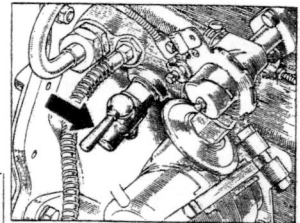

Left: shows cylinder bl... drain tap ...uated on the ... side of the eng... adjacent to ... distributor u...

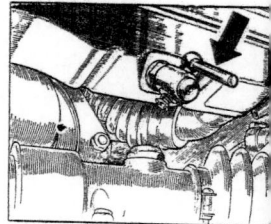

Right: shows the radiator drain tap at the base of the bottom tank on the nearside. Access from below

FILL-UP DATA

	Pints	Litres
Engine sump (including filter)	7	4.00
Gearbox	4	2.27
Rear axle	$2\frac{3}{4}$	1.56
Cooling system	10	5.67
Fuel tank	10 gal	45.4
Tyre pressures: front	17 lb/sq in	1.2 kg/cm²
rear	20 lb/sq in	1.4 kg/cm²

RECOMMENDED LUBRICANTS

		Duckham's	Wakefield	Esso	Mobil	Shell	B.P. Energol	Filtrate	Sternol
Engine oil bath, air cleaner	Above 32°F	NOL 30	Castrol XL	"Esso" Extra Motor Oil 20W/30	Mobiloil A	X-100 30	Energol SAE 30	Medium Filtrate 30	WW 30
	32°–0°F	NOL 20	Castrolite		Mobiloil Arctic	X-100 20/20W	Energol SAE 20W	Zero Filtrate 20	WW20
	Below 0°F	NOL 10	Castrol Z	Essolube 10	Mobiloil 10W	X-100 10W	Energol SAE 10W	Sub Zero Filtrate 10	WW 10
Gearbox	All temperatures	NOL 30	Castrol XL	Essolube 30	Mobiloil A	X-100 30	Energol SEA 30	Medium Filtrate 30	WW 30
Rear axle, steering, gearbox	Above 10°F	Hypoid 90	Castrol Hypoy	Esso Expee Compound 90	Mobilube GX 90	Spirax EP 90	Energol EP SAE 90	Hypoid Filtrate Gear 90	Ambroleum EP 90
	Below 10°F	Hypoid 80	Castrol Hypoy 80	Esso Expee Compound 80	Mobilube GX 80	Spirax EP 80	Energol EP SAE 80	Hypoid Filtrate Gear 80	Ambroleum EP 80
Wheel hubs, fan bearings		LB.10 Grease *	Castrolease L.M. *	Esso Multi-Purpose Grease "H" *	Mobilgrease M.P.	Retinax A	Energrease L3	Super Lithium Filtrate Grease	Ambroline LHT Grease
Chassis nipples, dynamo, cables, control joints		LB.10 Grease	Castrolease L.M.	Esso Multi-Purpose Grease "H"	Mobilgrease M.P.	Retinax A	Energrease L3	Super Lithium Filtrate Grease	Ambroline LHT Grease
Brake fluid: Lockheed Orange									

*Latest rec.: no alternatives